Executing Global Projects

Executing Global Projects

A Practical Guide to Applying the PMBOK Framework in the Global Environment

James W. Marion and Tracey M. Richardson

BEP BUSINESS EXPERT PRESS

Executing Global Projects: A Practical Guide to Applying the PMBOK Framework in the Global Environment

Cover Image Credit: violetkaipa/shutterstock.com

First published in 2020 by
Business Expert Press, LLC
222 East 46th Street, New York, NY 10017
www.businessexpertpress.com

ISBN-13: 978-1-94999-173-4 (paperback)
ISBN-13: 978-1-94999-172-7 (e-book)

Business Expert Press Portfolio and Project Management Collection

Collection ISSN: 2156-8189 (print)
Collection ISSN: 2156-8200 (electronic)

Cover and interior design by Exeter Premedia Services Private Ltd., Chennai, India

First edition: 2020

10 9 8 7 6 5 4 3 2 1

Printed in the United States of America.

Abstract

Project management is a discipline that is practiced in today's organizations on a global scale. The project manager's role has therefore become more complex as projects are carried out in different geographical locations using team members who come from a diverse range of languages, cultures, and worldviews. Project managers improve their chances of success when they seek to understand the cultures and context of the environment with which they interact on a day-to-day basis and modify the way they manage, communicate, and organize. This book identifies some of the most significant complexities faced by project managers when attempting to implement the PMBOK framework in global projects and provides pointers for existing or aspiring managers and project managers. Further, a framework is proposed for assessing and building global project capability and process maturity.

Keywords

project; project management; global project management; culture; customs; global process capability

Contents

Contents

PART I

Strategy and Planning in the Global Project Context

CHAPTER 1

Starting and Planning the Global Project

What is so special about projects that are planned and executed within the global environment? Why should project managers concern themselves with examining global projects as something distinct from projects that are purely local, regional, or national in scope? This question may be answered in a single word—*complexity*. Global projects include significantly more variables to manage including the macroenvironment. The global macroenvironment is vast and includes the political, economic, social, and technological factors in which a global project is executed. Further, project managers encounter language and cultural barriers that often involve fundamentally different approaches to management itself. To make an analogy, when project managers face such factors, it is rather like attempting to drive a car from one location to another while wearing a blindfold. The environment faced by the project manager may be quite alien, thereby leading to confusion, miscommunication, conflict, and stress. On the other hand, when project managers take the time to understand the global project management environment and become more comfortable with the added complexity, it is not uncommon to find global project management to be a successful and rewarding experience (Figure 1.1).

Whether a project manager desires to lead a global project or not, projects today are increasingly global in scope. Often an apparently purely local project will include some components, subsystems, software, technology, or labor sourced from outside of the home country. As a result, even local project managers may be required to communicate with or travel to suppliers who are outside of the home country. These requirements present little problem since modern technology has made it possible to communicate in real time anywhere on the globe. Further, jet travel

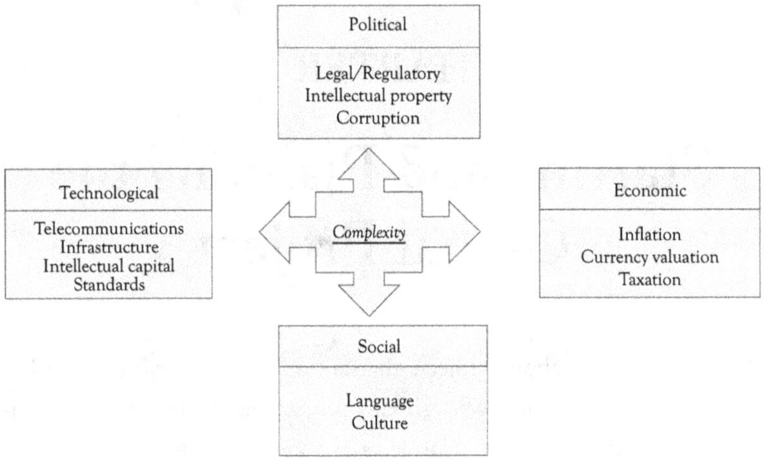

Figure 1.1 The global project management environments

makes it possible to travel from any major city in the world to any other major city in less time than it was required to travel between the original Greek city states in antiquity. The world is effectively smaller—but since the world is round and it is not physically smaller, the apparent smallness enables global projects but leaves the additional stresses, strains, and complexities in place. Jumping into a global project without serious consideration of the many facets of the global macroenvironment is much like planning a project that includes a significant component of scope that is hidden and not revealed until later in the project. There is more at stake, more at risk, and more for the project manager to do in a global project than any project that is carried out on a purely local scale.

Complexity = Risk

The many additional factors that a global project manager must consider effectively increases the overall project risk. Like any project risk uncovered by the project team, the risks associated with the global environment may be identified, analyzed, ranked, and linked to appropriate risk responses. Given the special nature of the global macroenvironment, a separate and distinct "global risk register" may be created to track and keep an ongoing appraisal of global risks. Further, in large-scale projects—which global

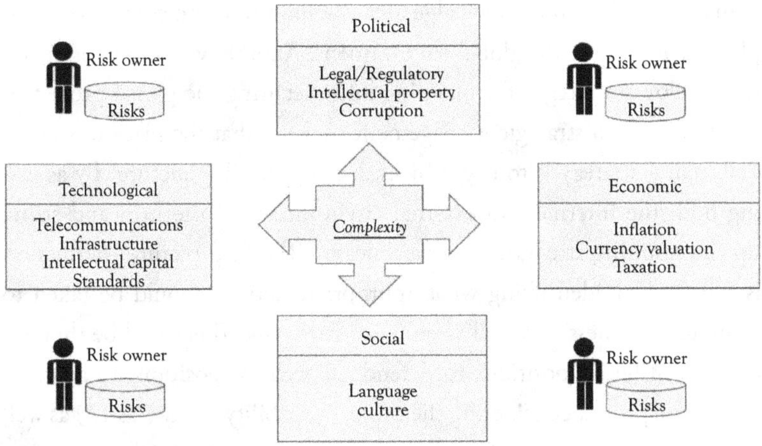

Figure 1.2 Global risk and risk owners

projects often are—it is recommended to have a project team member assigned to "own" and lead the project team in managing these risks (Figure 1.2).

One reason for approaching global project risks in this manner is that the logistics of implementing risk responses is likely to be far more complex than that involved in purely localized risk responses. It is simpler to call a meeting with local suppliers to resolve an issue, but addressing problems with suppliers and contractors in Eastern Europe, India, and Asia—at the same time—presents unique difficulties. The scale of global risks that materialize into issues are likely to reach the scope of a major subproject. It is for this reason that in-depth global project risk identification, risk analysis, and risk response scenario planning is assigned to and carried out by the owner of the global project risk register.

Start with "SWOT the PEST"

The Guide to the Project Management Body of Knowledge (PMBOK) includes knowledge areas associated with each discipline required for carrying out each of the process groups. There is no single process group associated with managing a project within the global environment—but perhaps there should be. At minimum, a project team could create, as is required in most knowledge areas, a "plan for a plan," that is, a strategy for managing each of the knowledge area disciplines in the context of complexities unique to the global environment. Another way of saying this is to "develop a strategy" for planning and executing the global project. A good practice in strategic management suggests that the place to start in developing strategy is to begin by evaluating the "big picture" by assessing both the internal and external environment of the firm and sizing up the resulting strengths and weaknesses. The "big picture" evaluation is followed by identifying what appropriate actions should be taken to shore up weaknesses as well as enhance strengths. This could be thought of as identifying "positions to defend" as well as "positions to achieve" within the project considering the project capability today ("as-is") as well as where the project needs to be in the future ("to-be"). The process of global strategy development within the project environment need not differ significantly from that of the firm—the primary exception being the temporary nature of the project as well as its focus on producing tangible deliverables.

The Big Picture

The big picture view of strategy begins with the analysis of the Strengths, Weaknesses, Opportunities, and Threats, or SWOT analysis of the project as it faces the global macroenvironment. A mnemonic device for SWOT analysis in global projects is the phrase "SWOT the PEST," or the evaluation of "Strengths, Weaknesses, Opportunities and Threats in light of the Political, Economic, Social and Technological environment" in which the project is planned and executed. In the corporate environment, a SWOT analysis is focused on attaining and maintaining a competitive advantage. In the global project environment, "SWOTting the PEST" is all about understanding the capabilities, liabilities, opportunities, and vulnerabilities given the additional factors afforded by the global environment. One approach to doing this is to carry out a brainstorming session where each PMBOK knowledge area is analyzed using a SWOT analysis with a special focus on PEST. A generic example of the output of this process is provided in Table 1.1 (Project Management Institute 2017).

Upon completion of the SWOT analysis, the project team makes an assessment of the special focus and possible additional action that must

Table 1.1 SWOT analysis of PMBOK knowledge areas

Knowledge Area	Strength	Weakness	Opportunity	Threat
Integration		Process differences Decision making		
Scope		Change management process		Hidden additional scope
Schedule				
Cost				Travel, communication, currency valuation
Quality				
Resources		Virtual team management	Software development teams: India, Eastern Europe	
Communication		Language, Culture	Intranet application, Skype implementation	Misunderstanding
Risk				
Procurement		Logistics		Taxes, duties
Stakeholders		Geographical distance		

be taken in developing subplans associated with each knowledge area. As a first step, the project team can consider what modification may be required for the management of each knowledge area by asking specific questions that will be answered in the associated plans that are developed. These questions are developed in the global project knowledge area walkthrough.

Global Project Strategy Process

Project management is known to have borrowed process support from operations management. One example of this is the quality management processes that are consistent with quality policies in operations. Likewise, the global project team may consider borrowing processes from strategic management to more fully consider how to strategically produce an effective plan that successfully addresses global risks. The first step in the strategic management process is *analysis*. The analysis phase is characterized by the SWOT analysis to understand those global factors of concern within each process. The analysis phase may be concluded with a workshop that reviews the findings of the SWOT analysis.

Global Project Knowledge Area Walk-Through

A walk-through of each knowledge area may be accomplished using techniques used in project planning workshops. Instead of identifying and sequencing activities, the focus is on identifying questions that each element of the global project plan must answer, as follows:

Integration

Who will participate in the development of the overall project plan, and how will globally distributed teams contribute to it?
What decisions will need to be made in the development of the project plan, and to what extent will local teams participate in such decisions?
What language, culture, or distance barriers stand in the way of developing the overall project plan?

Scope

What additional elements of scope would need to be added because of international standards? What legal and standards-based factors must be included in the scope of the project?
How will the project requirements be collected?
How will trade-offs between local and global scope requirements be managed?
How will the integrated change control process function in an environment of globally distributed teams?

Schedule

To what extent does international logistics and travel impact the project schedule?

What impact will the difference in holidays and observances impact the project schedule?

Cost

What costs should be considered that go beyond typical expenditures for local projects?
In what currencies will costs be tabulated?
What commercial terms will the project team face that have the potential to increase project costs?

Quality

What quality standards must be considered when defining the project?
What regional differences in quality standards must be researched and evaluated?

Resources

From where should management and labor resources be sourced?
In what location(s) will capital and labor resources be housed?

Communication

What steps should be taken to avoid miscommunication given language differences?
When and how often should communication take place between the local and geographically dispersed teams?
What changes in timing of synchronous communication should be considered given different time zones?
Where and how often will face-to-face communication take place?

Risk

Will the project require additional insurance to deal with travel and extended local residence of team members?
What additional resources must be assigned to risk mitigation plans?
What measures must be undertaken in order to ensure the personal safety of team members around the world?

Procurement

From where will the project obtain hardware and software components, materials, and subcontractors?
What additional steps must be taken by the project to ensure quality of vendor-supplied components and labor?
How will the project team assess the financial health and process maturity of globally distributed suppliers?

Stakeholders

What high-power/high-interest stakeholders may exist in globally distributed locations about whom the project team is not currently aware?
How will stakeholders from different cultures and different languages be effectively engaged?

The project team, in the course of developing the global project plan, must carefully consider the questions raised in the knowledge area walk-through and ensure that the project plan sufficiently answers each of the questions.

Considering Options

The next stage in the strategic management process is *strategy formulation*. In global project management, this roughly equates to outlining several generic options that may be applied in responding to the risks identified in the analysis phase. One approach for considering response plan possibilities is to conduct scenario planning (Figure 1.3).

For every risk scenario, the project team creates several possible approaches to dealing with the risk. Further, an overriding risk philosophy or policy approach to various categories of identified risk may begin to gel. At the formulation stage, the more global project strategic risk response options available from which to select the better for the project.

Selecting Options

After analysis and formulation, the strategic management process requires a choice of strategy. In global project management terms, strategic choice

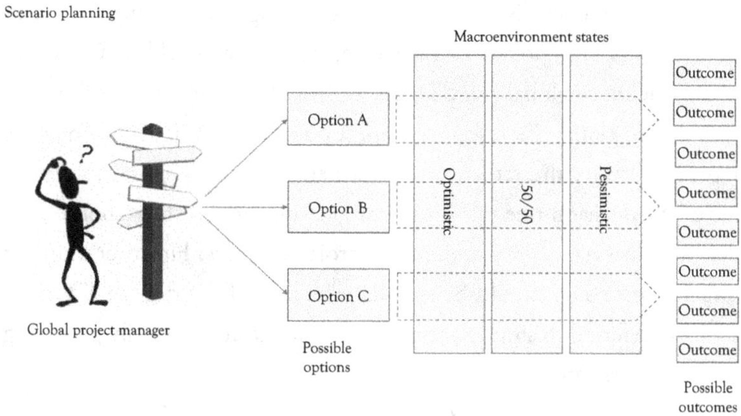

Figure 1.3 Global project scenario planning

equates to making decisions between alternative response scenarios. Deciding between several different risk response options can often be a daunting task. On the other hand, response options could be thought of as small projects. For this reason, it makes sense to employ techniques from the PMBOK that are designed for just this purpose. Project selection methods include both qualitative as well as quantitative methods. A qualitative approach, applying expert judgment, could employ a simple checklist that outlines what is of greatest concern to the global project team (Figure 1.4).

A checklist selects options by assuming equal weights

#	Response option	Observed benefit
✓	Replan subsystem development	*Utilize more mature technology*
✓	Scope reduction negotiation	*Reduce resources and project duration*
✓	Move development to new region	*Reduce labor and facility costs*
	Revise contract	*Achieve more favorable terms*

A weighted scoring model scores options and weights according to priority

Weight	Score	Total	Response option	Observed benefit
0.25	11.25	45	Replan subsystem development	*Utilize more mature technology*
0.3	19.5	65	Scope reduction negotiation	*Reduce resources and project duration*
0.4	24	60	Move development to new region	*Reduce labor and facility costs*
0.1	7.5	75	Revise contract	*Achieve more favorable terms*

Figure 1.4 A weighted scoring model for global projects

Further, the checklist could evolve to a weighted ranking matrix in which weights are applied to each element of the checklist. Quantitative approaches to global risk plan decision-making consider the financial aspects of the global risk response plan. A quantitative analysis such as the net present value, the return on investment, or the expected monetary value of the decision tree inform the project manager if the response generally produces gains greater than the projected costs. However, the cost of the response plan should be less than the cost of the risk itself. Otherwise, it is preferred to simply accept the risk without necessarily preparing an extended response plan.

Implementation

The final stage of the strategic management process is strategy implementation. This stage involves putting in motion the strategies that were decided from analysis, formulation, and choice. The analog in the context of global project management is to charter subprojects designed to plan and implement responses to global risk scenarios. Since in each case the plans are addressing risks (rather than risks that have materialized to become *issues*), implementation at this stage may be as simple as creating subproject charters and accompanying scope statements to have on standby should they become necessary to employ.

What Would a Global Project Knowledge Area Look Like?

A knowledge area within the PMBOK that provided specific process support for managing global projects would guide project teams to identify and understand the unique elements of a global project that require significant planning and close management. Further, such a knowledge area would direct teams to assess their own fitness and any necessary corrective action for managing the global project. Finally, the knowledge area would direct the team to develop plans for managing global project factors with emphasis on risk management. An additional knowledge area for the global environment would provide guidance on the development of project subplans to address the impact presented by additional global factors,

Table 1.2 A global project management knowledge area

Global project factor management	Description
Identify global project factor impacts	Identify impact to the project of distance, culture, language, social, political, and regulatory matters.
Conduct global project SWOT analysis	Assess Strengths, Weaknesses, Opportunities, and Threats associated with the global Political, Economic, Social, and Technological Environment
Plan management of global project factors	Identify and select strategy for managing identified global project factors
Identify global risk factors	Identify specific risks unique to the global project environment
Plan global risk factor responses	Develop plans resulting from evaluating risk scenarios and developing and selecting strategies for addressing global risks.

and as well, identify, analyze, and plan risk responses for risks unique to the global environment (Table 1.2)

Risks Unique to the Global Environment

The political and legal environment will naturally differ from country to country. This means that a project team creating the plan must be familiar with local regulations. In some environments, the legal environment proves so daunting that local legal representation including contact with local government officials will be required. An example of this is in carrying out a project within a country led by a strong central government such as the People's Republic of China. In this context, if the project involves construction, installation, or long-term stays of any kind, local legal representation with ties to local and regional government is a must. There is no substitute for local know-how when it comes to the regulatory and legal environment in which the project interacts. Never assume that the details of the local environment can be understood and adapted to by carrying out cursory research on the subject. It is also important to remember that project managers working in a different country are guests of that country and should take care not to cause offense (Figure 1.5).

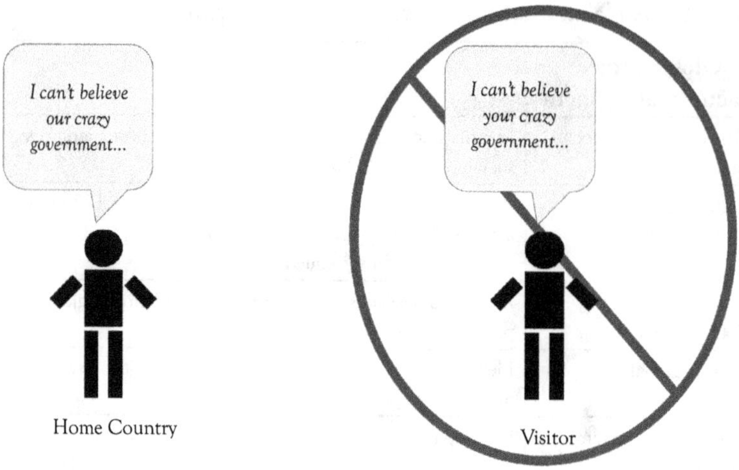

Figure 1.5 What not to say when visiting another country

Example of Unintended Offense

A classic example of the potential to cause unintended offense could be illustrated by the pitfalls of using the wrong terminology when doing business in the People's Republic of China. In the People's Republic of China, it is considered an insult to the government to refer to Taiwan in formal or informal communication as the Republic of China (ROC). The People's Republic of China in Mainland China does not recognize Taiwan as being an independent republic. Therefore, simply mentioning it can cause great offense and can lead to the ejection of the project team from the country. This is an example of an unintended political insult that can cause significant friction. Although it is common when traveling to other countries to find that the locals are perfectly content to work together with Western project managers, there may be considerable political differences that exist between the country being visited and the project team country of origin. There is an old saying that "…one should never discuss religion and politics in church." Global project managers should keep this in mind and particularly avoid opinionated conversations about political trends, the activities of different governments, or religious differences. If project team members do encounter criticism of the home country, its political leaders, religion, or culture, it is best to let it pass without comment.

Personal Safety

The personal safety of project team members when travelling the globe on project business cannot be taken for granted. The international environment may present challenges for personal safety that may not exist to the same degree in the home country. Safety concerns may involve crime, but other concerns exist as well and include fundamental concerns such as the presence of disease and the lack of food safety due to unsanitary conditions. Other more fundamental physical concerns such as extreme heat, cold, or excessive humidity may present unexpected challenges if not considered in advance. There may also be significant seasonal changes depending upon the hemisphere destination. Prior to sending anyone to another country for work on a project consider such factors as possible risks to personal safety. Examine reports published by the State Department and the Center for Disease Control on the state of crime, terrorism, and other physical and health concerns for personal safety to expect in the given country. Also confirm with a local doctor what vaccinations and medications should be used by the project team member before or perhaps during travel.

The PMBOK Versus International Standards

Using the knowledge areas of the PMBOK can be very useful to capture in detail how risk associated with international project management can impact the project. However, using the knowledge areas as a means for organizing risk analysis reflects the fact that the team is using the PMBOK framework as the primary reference standard for project planning and execution. It should be acknowledged though that not all project teams around the world will be as immersed in the PMBOK as a team that is based in the Western world, particularly the United States. Many different project management frameworks exist around the globe. The Global Alliance of Project Management Professionals (GAPP) seeks to coordinate and consolidate the different project management standards that do exist so that global project managers may be aware of the different standards. An inspection of the GAPP website illustrates that differences exist between project management standards around the world. It is also evident that there are many commonalities. In all cases projects must be started, planned, executed, monitored, controlled, and closed—even though the terminology associated with this sequence may differ. Also, even though the PMBOK outlines 10 knowledge areas with specific skill requirements for managing each of the process groups. Such skill requirements are not uncommon in most of the international standards. Two of the more common international project management standards include PRINCE2 and the International Project Management Association standard (Figure 1.6) (Global Alliance for the Project Professions 2019).

The fact that fundamental differences in project management standards suggests that the team leading the global project should take time to meet with local teams in order to agree upon which standard will be used and, if necessary, harmonize an approach to developing the global plan. Just as importantly, the team leading the global project should not assume that globally distributed teams, partners, or suppliers follow the same project standard that the team in the head office follows. Finally, an awareness of the terminology and the process steps employed in global project standards may help with the translation process when communicating the project lifecycle and the governance process. It is possible that different project management standards may use different terminology for commonly used processes. Developing an understanding of the differences in terminology may help considerably in reducing confusion and miscommunication.

Plan Review and Kick-Off

A general rule of thumb for developing a project plan is that for a plan to be effective, those charged with carrying out the plan must have a role in developing it. In the purely local environment, this is rarely challenging. Most of the high-level planning may be carried out by a co-located project team within the setting of a planning workshop. How does this work in the global environment? There are multiple ways of addressing this. First, the planning documentation as it is developed may be stored on an intranet site in which all distributed teams have access (Figure 1.7).

When updates occur, all local teams are alerted and directed to the updated plan and change log via a link. In addition to frequent

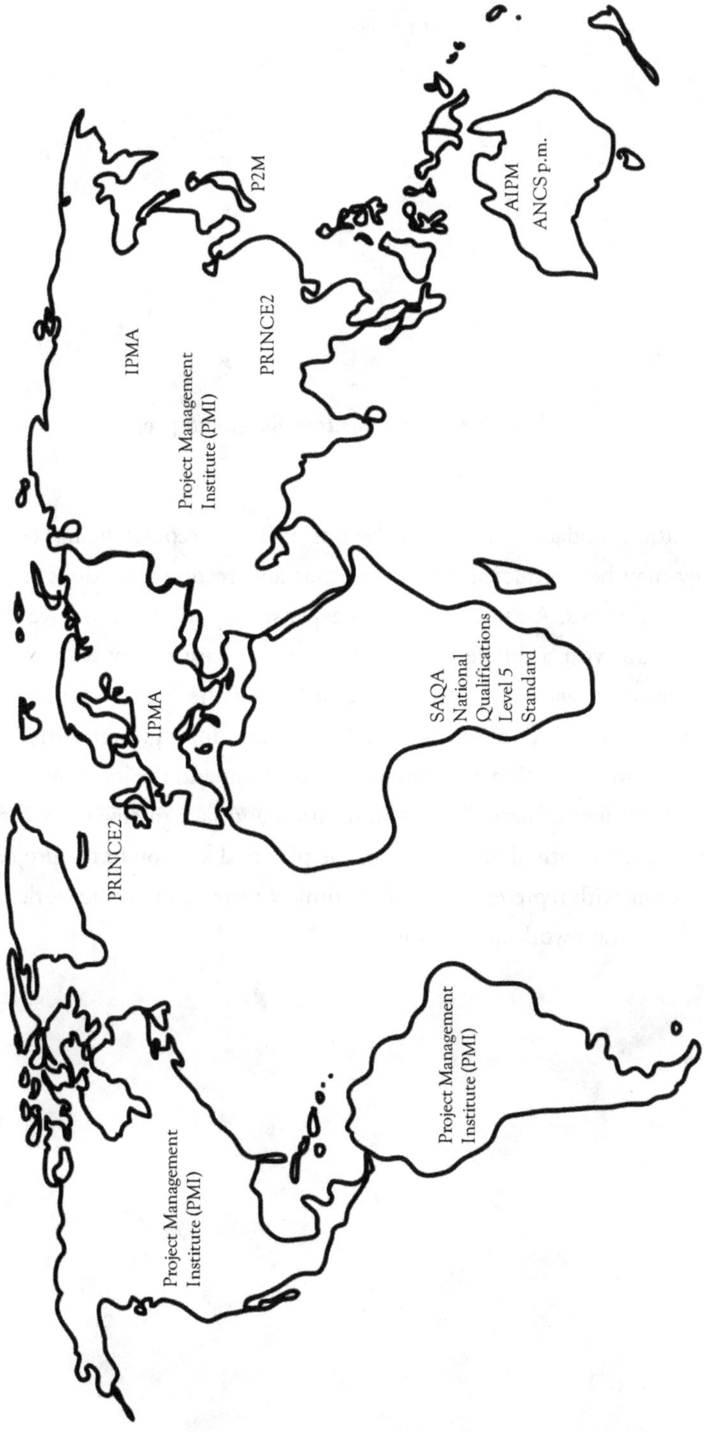

Figure 1.6 Global project management standards

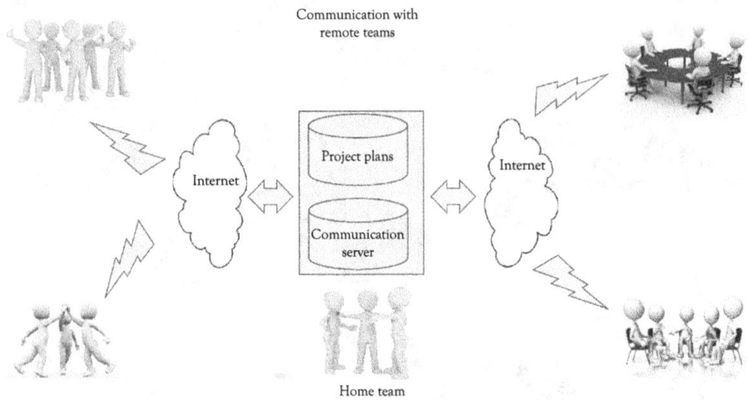

Figure 1.7 Central project plan repository for global projects

information updates, virtual workshops using teleconferencing technology may be conducted to collect input and recommendations from distributed teams. A more taxing and expensive approach is to have the project team visit a different local site at each phase review with other sites joining in via teleconference. Regardless of the logistic difficulties of this approach, it does provide the opportunity for a greater degree of feedback and interaction between the project team and the local environment. Regardless of periodic communication and face-to-face visits with local teams, the formal final review of the plan and kick-off of the project is best done with representatives of the project teams around the world in a single-location workshop setting.

PART II

Executing the Project

The PMBOK emphasizes project planning above all other process groups. This is evident in the number of processes dedicated to planning. The monitoring and controlling process group comes next when process groups are arranged in order of the number of processes they are made up of. Implicit in the relationship between the two groups are that plans are made, and then the plans are controlled. Planning in the global environment is extensive given the wide array of additional variables. It is a challenge to monitor and control each element of such a plan, but a more significant challenge lies in its execution. What does a global project manager do when executing a global project? What barriers to success may exist in its execution? One approach to answering these questions is to perform a walk-through of processes in the executing process group to better understand how the global environment impacts project execution. This walk-through mirrors the analysis of the knowledge areas carried out in the planning stage of the project.

CHAPTER 2

Executing Processes in the Global Environment

There are 10 processes allocated to the executing process group. How each process is managed will differ based upon the project scale, geography, language, and culture. The project team must be prepared to answer questions that are certain to arise when considering how to execute the plan in the global environment. A table of executing processes along with questions to be answered so that the execution of the project is supported is provided in Table 2.1 (Project Management Institute 2017).

Each of the issues raised in the walk-through of execution processes can be distilled into concerns about distance, trust, culture, and the global legal and regulatory environment.

Distance and Time Lag

A project that is global in scope usually involves globally distributed teams and more likely than not virtual teams. This arrangement takes away the intimacy and intensity of day-to-day face-to-face interaction that normally occurs when teams are co-located in the same venue. Even though jet travel and modern telecommunications lower the effective distance, the distance reveals itself in the time lag required for physical interaction, the differences in time zones, and finally, the implications on trust between team members. The time lag between locations has a tangible impact on project team members. To provide an example, assume that a project manager is based on the east coast of the United States. When this project manager is arriving at work, teams in Europe are going to lunch, whereas teams in Asia, if not still in the office, are at home or having dinner. Later in the evening on the east coast, the project manager may have a late-night conference call with Asian teams. The daily work of the project manager

Table 2.1 Global project questions in the Executing process group

Processes within the executing process group	Global project questions to be answered
Direct and manage project work	What kind of oversight and supervision of project work carried out in geographically distant locations is required? How will project work be assigned to geographically dispersed teams?
Manage project knowledge	How will lessons learned be captured and organized from geographically distributed operations? What standards will be used for language, document formatting, nomenclature, and storage of information?
Manage quality	What quality standards will the project employ? How will quality be assured and controlled as components and subassemblies from remote operations are integrated? Who will manage and make decisions regarding the quality of project deliverables?
Acquire resources Develop team Manage team	From where will resources be obtained? What language-, cultural-, or distance-related factors should be considered when building, training, and supervising geographically distributed teams? How will virtual teams be managed?
Manage communications	What language and cultural considerations must be considered in the choice of media, location, frequency, and language of information exchange?
Implement risk responses	How are global risk plans triggered and managed once risks become issues?
Conduct procurements	From where we will source labor, hardware, and software components, and capital equipment in geographically distant locations? How do we ensure the performance of remote vendors? Who authorizes procurements in remote locations? What legal jurisdiction will govern globally distributed contracts?
Manage stakeholder engagement	What special measures must be considered for conducting meetings, project reviews, and negotiations given the impact of language, culture, and distance?

is therefore "bookended" by early morning and late-night conference calls with geographically distributed teams. A global project manager could therefore be thought of as having a never-ending "round-the-clock" job.

Figure 2.1 The long day of the project manager

The time effect created by distance also has significant implications for travel to face-to-face meetings. When the same project manager on the east coast of the United States travels to continental Europe for meetings, the flight will typically leave in the evening, cross the Atlantic through an unusually short evening, followed by a morning arrival. The first day unfolds as an ongoing battle to remain awake given the time shift and the short evening. Given the grind of the first day of jet lag, it is usually not difficult to fall asleep. However, when the alarm goes off at 6 a.m. the following morning, the project manager's watch will indicate midnight. Waking up at this hour can be a daunting prospect. The project manager going into an important decision-making meeting should be aware that he or she may not be capable of clear thinking or communications. It is easy to make mistakes in such a situation (Figure 2.1).

On the other hand, when an east coast project manager travels to Asia for meetings, flying over is like a very long day. The plane follows the sun across the Pacific Ocean and lands in the afternoon. It is not unusual for project managers to wake up fully refreshed around 4 to 5 a.m. the next morning. The feeling is like staying up all night and sleeping throughout the following day. What implications exist for traveling east versus west for important project meetings? It is generally easier to attend an important morning meeting overseas when traveling west than it is when traveling east. If you have an important project negotiation meeting approaching and you have a choice of venue, prefer to go west.

Intranet and Calendar

The fact that the project operates across large geographical distances makes it implicit that many of the teams working on the project will be virtual teams. Virtual team members do not usually interact with each other on a day-to-day basis. It is important then for the project manager to ensure that team members are familiar with the names of each team member, where they are located, their contact information, and finally, the time zones they inhabit. As a suggestion, creating intranet page for the project team and subpages for every localized project team around the world would foster familiarity and trust between globally distributed team members (Figure 2.2).

It is further recommended that information about every team member be published on the site and include with this project team a calendar that provides the current time in every project location. This aids in the coordination of conference calls and as well duly noting holidays and vacation periods to minimize confusion and inconvenience.

Distance and Trust

It is easier to trust project team members who are co-located in the same facility. This is natural given the constant interaction of co-located

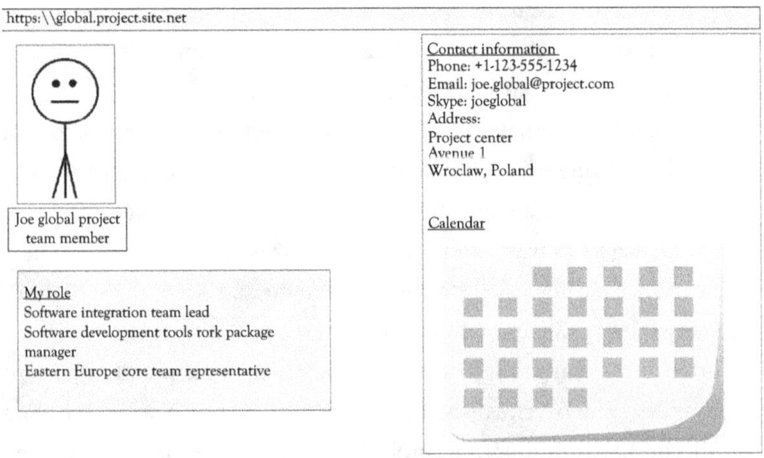

Figure 2.2 Intranet pages for project teams and team members

employees. The strength of trust between project teams and team members tends to be inversely proportional to the distance involved. It could be said that trust itself need not be extended in co-located teams since a follow-up on commitments may be carried out immediately. A "trust but verify" approach works well when verification of deliverables is a trivial matter. However, trust takes considerable effort to develop when verification and oversight is not so trivial. The further the physical distance, the less likely it is that the project team will be willing to assign important work without extensive controls in place. Further, physical distance is but one element of the trust equation. Differences in language, culture, and management of processes effectively increase the distance between project teams, thereby decreasing the level of trust. Project teams can learn lessons in developing trust by examining applications that are designed to create trust between users who are separated by physical distance. One familiar application in common use among globally distributed stakeholders is eBay. Consumers bid for products, they pay money to sellers when they win the bid, and they trust sellers to deliver the product as described. How is trust developed? By use of the feedback mechanism. Bidders trust sellers who have higher positive ratings. Project managers may consider ways to put feedback in place to develop a stronger performance track record. Projects are not likely to have a built-in review system such as eBay, but they can implement simple electronic survey and polling systems to collect frequent feedback and thereby build trust.

Trust and Distance Revisited

Since distance reduces trust between geographically distributed team members, one approach to building trust is to remove the distance—at least initially and perhaps periodically. As a practical example, consider bringing together representatives of the global teams involved in the project for a kick-off scheduling and team-building workshop. Time spent together in a workshop environment may aid in building initial trust relationships that aid in facilitating the day-to-day work at a distance (Figure 2.3).

Further, bringing together distributed team members periodically for project review and planning meetings helps to solidify trust relationships.

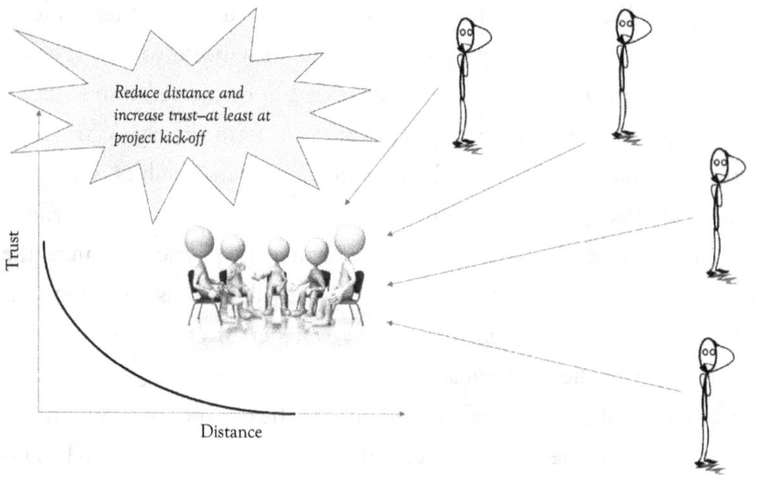
Reduce distance and
increase trust–at least at
project kick-off
Trust
Distance

Figure 2.3 The relationship between trust and distance

Although working at a distance and working within virtual teams is the norm within the information age in which we live, this does not infer that face-to-face meetings are to be ruled out completely. Face-to-face encounters may never be a frequent possibility, but offering the opportunity for face-to-face interaction from time to time has the potential to minimize or eliminate miscommunication, a mismatch of expectations, and conflict.

Distance and Management

It is observed that lack of trust between teams separated by physical distances makes it much more difficult for project managers to lead remote teams and guarantee affective outputs. How then should project managers approach managing geographically distributed teams? Mintzberg provides clarity in this matter by providing a framework for managing and coordinating teams. Four general methods are outlined by Mintzberg: (i) mutual adjustment, (ii) standardization, (iii) direct supervision, and (iv) informal coalitions. Of the four, direct supervision is not possible when managing teams over remote distances. In the absence of clear policy directives, the project manager and the distributed teams may gradually adjust to each other and ultimately find a reasonable means for working together. Also, in the absence of clear policies, globally distributed teams

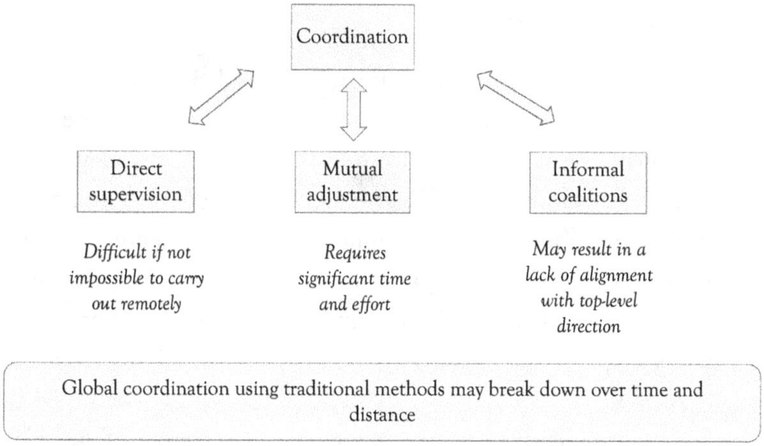

Figure 2.4 The difficulty of traditional coordination methods

may begin to work together and gradually begin jointly asserting their own preferences for managing work and producing project deliverables (Figure 2.4).

Given the difficulty of managing in an environment of mutual adjustment and coalitions as well as the physical impossibility of direct supervision, the project manager is left with standardization as the primary means for governing globally distributed teams. The question becomes, "standardize what?" Mintzberg proposes methods for coordinating work that could potentially be applied to global teams.

Standardization of Work Processes

The first of the suggested means for standardization is the standardization of "work processes." Given that teams in different global regions may have their own standards and processes, and the direct supervision is not possible in the global project team environment, standardization using common work processes may not be the most viable approach for the global project manager. Mintzberg further proposes standardization of skills and knowledge. Skills and knowledge are important for producing quality project deliverables; however, skills and knowledge could be considered inputs to the process rather than outputs. Therefore, skills and knowledge do not necessarily equate to excellent performance outcomes.

Standardization of Norms

Norms may also be used to standardize how work is done across the globe. Norms work well only if all distributed team members are well-versed in such norms. This is usually the case when all team members are part of the same culture. But, it does not work in the global environment. Project team members at the head office may share a common culture and associated norms; so, the team should not assume that team members distributed around the globe are familiar with the same set of norms. When this happens, it often leads to false assumptions and miscommunication. A classic example of the result of the mismatch in norms is when Japanese companies carry out projects and operations outside of the home country. Japanese nationals are steeped in the norms of their culture and their country. Team members who are geographically distant typically will not exhibit such norms and further they may not even be aware of them. The resulting mismatch of expectations and frustration has long been observed to create havoc in Japanese global operations. Standardization using norms is therefore difficult to implement in practice.

Standardization of Outputs

What then are global project managers left with to manage and coordinate project work on a global scale? The fourth and final standardization technique is given by Mintzberg as "standardization of outputs." This is a standardization method that lends itself to the management of global teams. Regardless of cultures, norms, and process differences, each team regardless of the location around the globe must produce deliverables that meet a clear, predefined standard. Such a standard could also be accompanied with checklists and detailed acceptance criteria. In terms of governance using such an approach, global teams could be charged with the execution of work packages to be delivered according to a clear scope standard and accompanied by a schedule and an associated budget. As long as the team meets the specified criteria within a specified tolerance, then the local team has a free rein to freely execute with minimal oversight. If the team determines that one or more elements of the agreed-on assignment cannot be met, then the local team calls for an oversight meeting to either cancel the work, revise it, or reassign it. The approach of

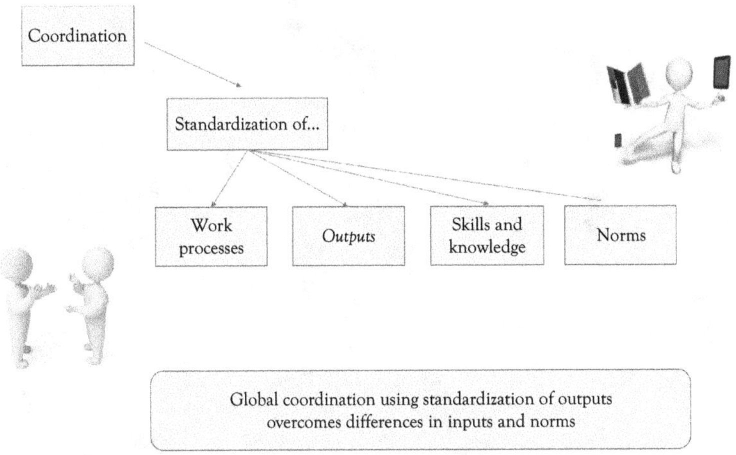

Figure 2.5 Global coordination by standardization

managing local geographically distributed project teams using this form of Mintzberg's standardization is less taxing on the team charged with the overall project responsibility and takes into account the common variability of inputs to project work products (Figure 2.5) (Mintzberg 1979).

Distant, but National

It is often the case that project managers lead large projects that involve multiple teams that are separated by physical distance—yet remain within the same country. Many of the principles of managing global projects apply. The "trust versus distance" concern applies whether the geographical distance does or does not cross international borders. Further, it is not uncommon for a single country to contain many different subcultures and different overall approaches to getting work done. Because of this, global project management principles offer many tools and techniques for building trust and coordinating work that could be just as easily applied in geographically dispersed national projects.

CHAPTER 3

Global Projects and the Value Chain

While Mintzberg provides general guidance for coordinating project activities at a distance, another approach is to consider which specific project functions will be located in distant geographical locations and which will be maintained close at hand at or near the home office of the project. A method for considering such activity assignment in detail is to borrow again from strategic operations management and to analyze project activities in terms of the value chain. The value chain analysis methodology decomposes an operation into primary and secondary activities and identifies the contribution of each to determine the value added by each activity as well as how it contributes to the overall profit margin. Another way to employ value chain analysis is to use it as a tool for mapping out the location of each value chain activity. A generic value chain (Figure 3.1) for an operation was originally conceived as a map of functions associated with a manufacturing operation. The value chain describes the acquisition of inputs from suppliers using inbound logistics, performing of work via operations, followed by sales, marketing, and service. The primary activities are complemented by support activities, which for an operation include infrastructure, human resources, technology development, and procurement (Porter 2001).

The value chain for a project will differ from that of an ongoing operation due to its temporary nature. Further, some important elements of project management that are considered support activities could be viewed as primary activities in the project work. These include activities that are associated with PMBOK knowledge areas and include human resources and procurement. Likewise, primary activities within the operational

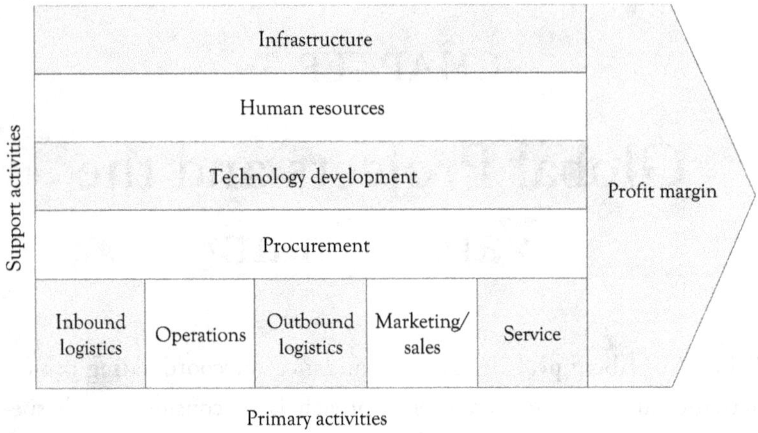

Figure 3.1 The value chain

context play more of a supporting role within the project management domain. These include marketing and sales as well as service. Although the project will communicate with marketing, sales, and service client stakeholders, the purpose of the interaction differs from that of an ongoing operation. For these reasons, these primary activities are moved to a supporting role. The value chain model for the project presented in Figure 3.2 better reflects actual project activities than that of the traditional value chain model for an operation.

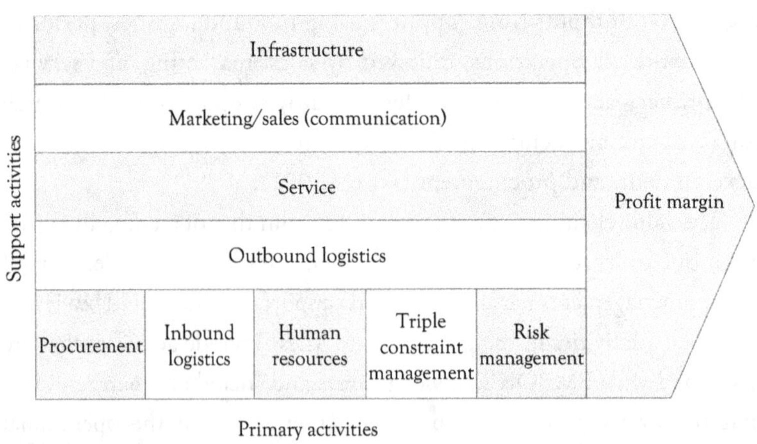

Figure 3.2 The project value chain

Location of Value Chain Elements

The rationale behind analyzing a global project using the value chain model is to aid in making decisions regarding the degree of centralization versus dispersion of each value chain function. In a purely local project, all elements of project value chain will be co-located as shown in Figure 3.3 or at minimum, located within the same country. In a global project, the completion of deliverables associated with the project scope may be distributed in virtual teams around the world. When this is the case, the operations element of the value chain will be distributed. Then, then the project will need to determine how functions such as procurement and inbound and outbound logistics will operate within the global environment. For example, will components, subsystems, or equipment flow through the project team in the head office? Or, will procurement and logistics functions be distributed throughout all global offices? Similar questions may be asked regarding the human resources function. Some elements of local team acquisition and management will of necessity be required in outlying operations. However, the project team will need to determine to what extent hiring policies and procedures from the sponsoring organization in the home country must be followed as well as how strictly. When some elements of the value chain are shared, the resulting value chain map will appear as given in Figure 3.3. When the

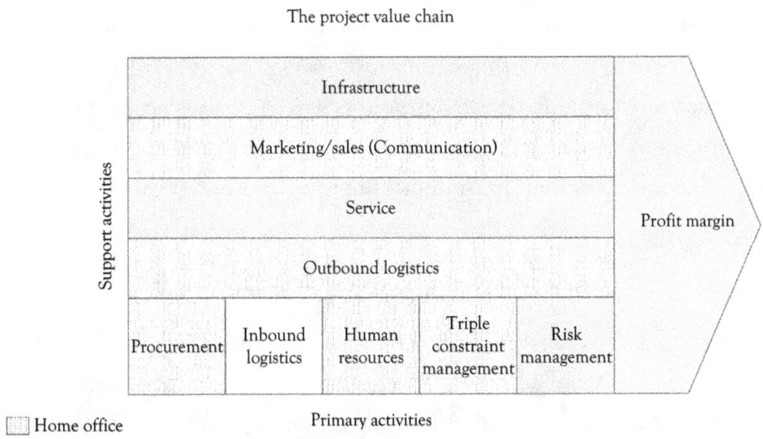

Figure 3.3 Project value chain elements allocated to home country

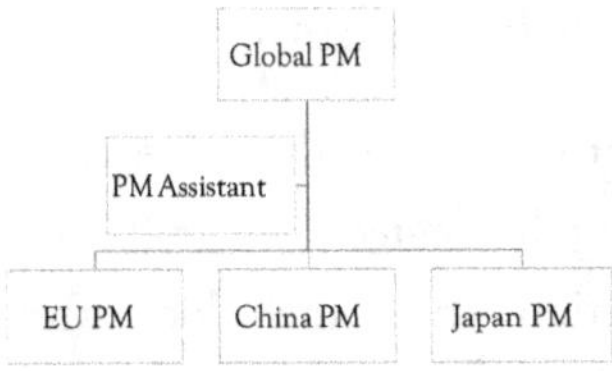

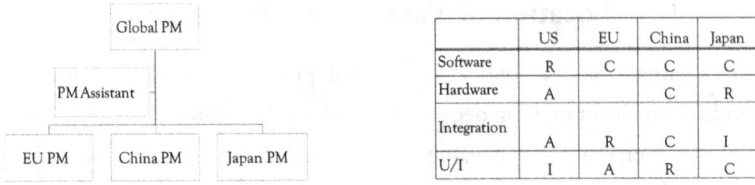

	US	EU	China	Japan
Software	R	C	C	C
Hardware	A		C	R
Integration	A	R	C	I
U/I	I	A	R	C

Responsible	Responsible for performing the task or creating the document
Accountable	Accountable and has sign-off authority for the task, such as the project manager, sponsor, technical lead
Consult	Providing expertise, advice, and support to the person responsible for the task or document and others
Inform	Informed of task progress or results, usually by the person responsible

Figure 3.4 Global project team RACI chart

global project value chain is managed in this way, clear boundaries and roles must be defined in documented processes.

A responsibility, accountability, consult, inform (RACI) chart may be used to clarify such roles and responsibilities as follows in Figure 3.4. A RACI chart employed in this manner is slightly different from the table used to assign individual project responsibilities. Instead of individuals, geographical locations are called out in the table. Also, instead of individual work packages, broad categories of work corresponding to value chain map elements are assigned to the geographical locations. This enables the understanding of the breakdown of responsibilities for each location. In addition to the RACI chart, an organization chart is useful for identifying reporting relationships. Such relationships may involve "solid lines" illustrating direct reporting authority, or "dotted lines" that describe matrixed relationships. The organization chart in this respect goes beyond assignment or value chain elements as its focus is on authority and reporting relationship so that decision making is streamlined (Figure 3.4).

Doing What Each Does Best

Operating in the global environment is particularly challenging when key responsibilities are allocated to those teams who can do the job regardless of where the team is located. Allocating global responsibilities in this way would appear to be ideal, yet it requires an extensive performance track

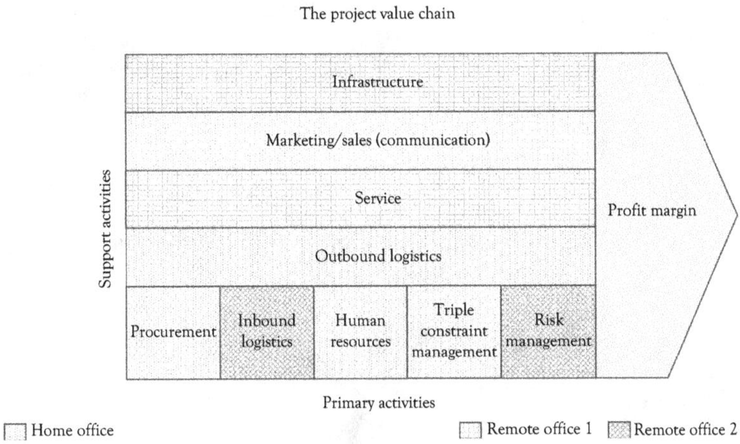

Figure 3.5 Value chain elements allocated to global locations

record as well as a deep sense of trust, which is often developed over many years. A project organized in this way may elect to focus the development of strategy and plans in the home office project team, but then tasks geographically dispersed teams with the realization of the plans, and other teams with functions such as transfer to manufacturing as well as distribution. A global team structured in this way would appear as in the value chain map as shown in Figure 3.5.

Regardless of the rationale that the global project team employs to distribute, coordinate, and manage work in the global environment, it is important to have such a rationale and to think it through in the planning stage of the project. Mintzberg's scheme for coordination of work as well as the value chain map are tools that function similarly to the risk breakdown (RBS) or organizational breakdown structure (OBS) in that they serve to stimulate ideas and thinking for the structure of global project execution.

CHAPTER 4

Context

Behaviors, norms, and customs form different patterns in different geographical regions around the world. Cultural differences therefore are an obvious concern for global project managers. Many frameworks exist to provide guidance on understanding global cultures and managing across cultures. One aspect of culture that is often overlooked by project managers is the role of context. Context refers to the degree to which situational assumptions govern communications and relationship versus explicitly communicating each detail. One lens for evaluating cultural difference is provided by the observation that some cultures tend to rely significantly on context when it comes to communications and relationships. When context is a significant component of cultural behaviors, much is left unsaid and instead communicated only indirectly. This is because a culture that relies heavily on context is embedded with a common set of assumptions. In this case, much less needs to be directly "spelled out." The context therefore plays a significant role in the communication channels when carrying out a global project. Some cultures may rely less on context and instead are explicit in communicating their views and requirements. What does this mean in practice for global project managers? When project managers interact with stakeholders from high-context cultures, communication is often less clear and more implicit. High-context communication tends to be less explicit because the context is used to carry a significant portion of the meaning (Figure 4.1).

High-context cultures therefore tend to insist on building strong relationships prior to conducting business and communicating meaningfully. The relationships provide the context of business and communication. As an example, a project manager should never expect to meet an overseas client from a high-context culture and expect to do business shortly after meeting for the first time. Important project decisions and negotiations are not something that is likely to be done quickly in a high-context

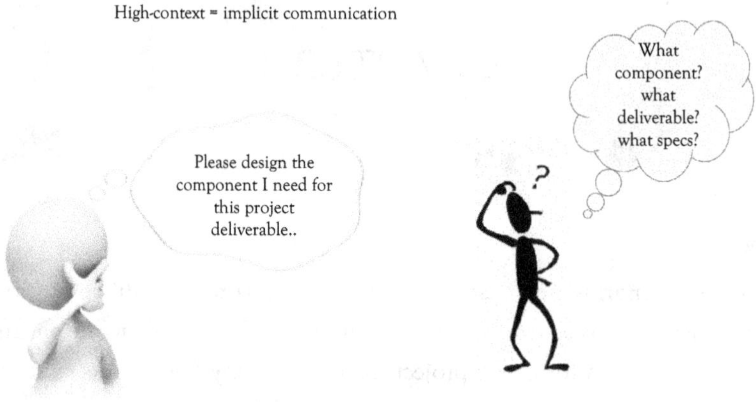

Figure 4.1 High-context and implicit communications

culture. Expect to spend time getting to know one another—perhaps on an informal basis—and then gradually "warm-up" to the prospect of doing business. To make an analogy, since the context is an essential to the communication, the "circuit" must be set up prior to communicating. In a telephone call, one must have a phone, and a connection, and then the communication takes place. In a high-context culture, the stage must be set with a personal relationship and a mutual understanding of the context. Then communications can flow. Asian cultures, including Japan, are said to be high-context cultures. Relationships and cultural norms play a key role in communicating important information that goes unsaid. Relationship-oriented business dealings are apparent in the web of *keiretsu* companies that work together in supplier, vendor, and financial relationships and they operate much like a family business. The emphasis on relationships rather than explicit documentation is evident in the number of lawyers per capita in Japan as compared to Western countries. Business that is done among friends and built from strong relationships can frequently be carried out on a handshake basis. Because of this, there is less reliance on letter of the law litigation among business parties.

Low-Context Culture

A low-context culture, by way of contrast, relies little on the context of the situation in order to conduct business. Neither relationship nor shared norms are assumed. Rather, the details of the engagement are spelled out in "black and white" using contractual arrangements. Whereas a high-context stakeholder may require a period of relationship building, a stakeholder from a low-context culture may be satisfied with an e-mail or a phone call. The low-context stakeholder drafts a written agreement that exhaustively documents all aspects of the engagement. Neither relationship nor norms are assumed or implied. Where would low-context cultures be found? Although Western countries in general tend to be lower in context than Asian countries, it is said that countries in northern Europe and Scandinavia are known to be representative of cultures significantly low in context than many others. It may be easier to strike a deal with the Scandinavian country by e-mail than with another country in Western Europe. This level of directness, brevity, and focus on the black-and-white again is not an option in high-context countries. High-context countries include many in Asia and Latin America that must be prepared with relationship building and face-to-face discussion prior to bringing up the subject of a possible business relationship.

High- and Low-Context Compared

The differences observed between high- and low-context cultures may be summed up with a series of simple observations. High-context cultures tend to communicate more implicitly versus explicitly. High-context cultures are often more relationship-oriented rather than task-oriented in their outlook. High-context cultures assume shared norms and assumptions and tend to prefer long-term business relationships. Finally, high-context cultures emphasize tacit versus explicit knowledge. Tacit knowledge is the knowledge embedded inside the mind of a co-worker or colleague. Since business relationships are often long-term rather than short-term in high-context cultures, knowledge tends to remain within organizations since employees tend to remain with an organization as part of lifetime employment. The concept of "knowledge management," which refers to the conversion of tacit knowledge to explicit knowledge as well as retaining knowledge when specific individuals leave the company, tends to be less of a concern within a high-context culture.

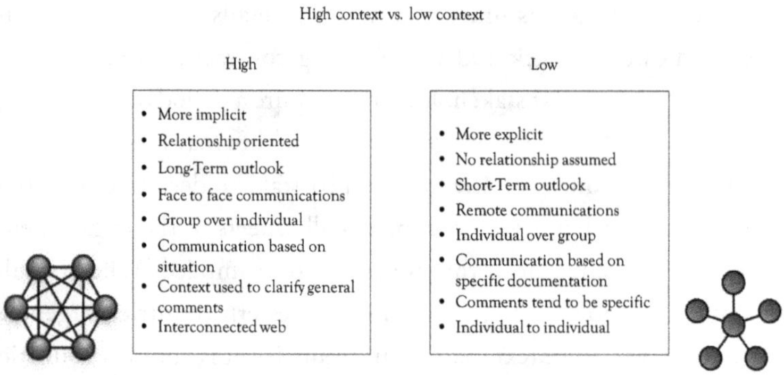

High context vs. low context
High
Low
• More implicit
• Relationship oriented
• Long-Term outlook
• Face to face communications
• Group over individual
• Communication based on situation
• Context used to clarify general comments
• Interconnected web
• More explicit
• No relationship assumed
• Short-Term outlook
• Remote communications
• Individual over group
• Communication based on specific documentation
• Comments tend to be specific
• Individual to individual

Figure 4.2 High- versus low-context

Low-context cultures favor documentation of rules, policies, procedures, and often communicate explicitly. Relationships are not assumed to be long term and this includes business relationships. Shared assumptions are not assumed, which infers that detailed and direct communication will be expected. Since knowledge in low-context cultures is explicit rather than tacit, it can be transferred more easily using documents, processes, and templates. Finally, low-context cultures will tend to prefer a task-oriented world-view (Figure 4.2) (Hall 1976).

Practical Implications of Context

Rushing too quickly into a high-context project relationship is a common mistake made by first-time global project managers. There is also the possibility of misunderstanding when communication is attempted between a low-context project manager and a high-context stakeholder (or vice versa). An example from Japan helps to illustrate this. In the absence of clearly established norms within a new relationship, the low-context norms will naturally be assumed by the Japanese stakeholder. The assumption of low-context Japanese management cultural norms is that the harmony of an interaction must be safeguarded at all costs. This may mean that if the Japanese stakeholder does not agree with a proposed policy, direction, or offering, the stakeholder may not openly say so. Instead, the Japanese stakeholder may appear to agree when agreement was never intended. This relates to the principles of *honne* and *tatamae. Honne* is the underlying truth of the matter, whereas *tatamae* is the "face" put on

Figure 4.3 Japanese–Western misunderstanding

a specific situation. Fellow Japanese nationals understand and interpret *honne* by observing facial expressions, tone of voice, and body language. However, Western nationals are not likely to understand this contextual channel of communication. Therefore, both parties are likely to separate with different understandings about what was agreed and what was not agreed to in the conversation (Figure 4.3).

This situation has additional implications when it comes to perspectives on project management and leadership. The Western, low-context tradition emphasizes the context of "integrity," which is "to mean what is said and to say what is meant." The Eastern, high-context view is "to mean what is communicated implicitly via the context, and to say what is most fitting in light of harmony preservation." The high-context view works well within its own cultural context. However, when high-context individuals communicate in this manner to low-context cultures, the low-context stakeholder will likely view the result in terms of "being told a lie." Likewise, when a low-context stakeholder communicates to a member of a high-context culture with presumption of "integrity," the resulting direct and often blunt communication will usually be viewed as immature and a sign of weak leadership. When preparing to discuss policy, procedure, documentation, work orders, or processes, consider carefully which parties in the discussion are high versus low context in outlook. Understanding this will aid the global project manager in communicating the direction more effectively.

Process and Context

It is observed that formal, explicitly documented process as well as the concept of process maturity is a characteristic of low-context culture. A high-context work environment where relationships and cultural norms prevail is likely to rely primarily on implicitly communicated processes. Further, a more informal approach to getting things done that draws upon mutual relationship is commonly observed in high-context cultures. In addition to this, the constraints associated with the process may be observed to be constrictive and problematic given that the context in which business exists is always changing. After all, why be locked into "hard and fast rules" when the context doesn't call for it? Japanese culture exhibits this in the concept of *chore bo kai*—the "short-lived" nature of making policy in the morning and proceeding to change it in the afternoon (Figure 4.4).

This relationship between process management and high versus low context provides an additional rationale for management and coordination by the standardization of outputs. A high-context culture that uses implicit norms and strong relationships to get things done rather than black-and-white process documentation is difficult to assess from a

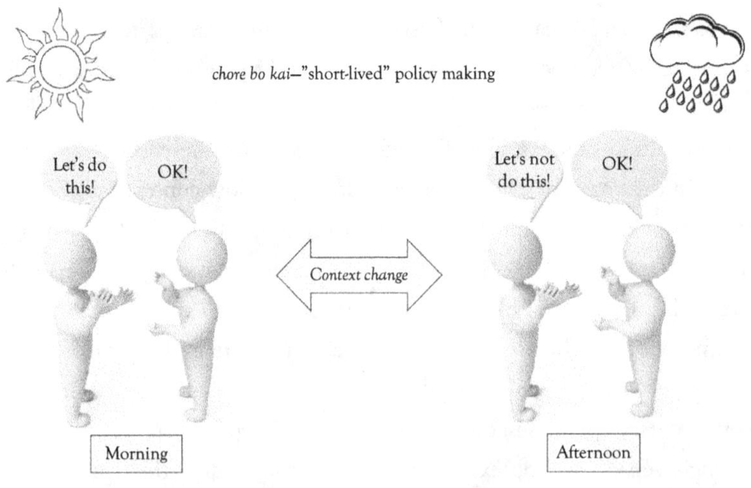

Figure 4.4 Context-dependent decision making

distance. It is by far more straightforward to evaluate outputs of the processes using predetermined and pre-communicated acceptance criteria. Finally, it pays for global project managers to understand which teams will assume implicit norms and shared values (high context) versus those who do not and will likewise be more accepting of policy and process direction (low context).

CHAPTER 5

Project Change Control

It is well known that Asian countries are the leading location for contract manufacturing for companies around the globe due to their excellence in manufacturing capability. One of the reasons for this is their culture of continuous improvement. The collectivist nature of culture, the intense face-to-face interaction on the manufacturing plant floor, and the willingness to work together for common good lead to an ongoing iterative cycle that follows Deming's guidance of *Plan-Do-Check-Act*. This is why Asian manufacturers often receive quality awards associated with their production of goods known to be extremely reliable. This continuous improvement outlook that works so successfully in manufacturing though may sometimes go astray within the project environment. The idea behind continuous improvement is often applied to the development of project requirements for the specification of deliverables in the project scope. While continuous improvement and process flow on the manufacturing floor is something that is tangible and always provides a positive contribution to quality and efficiency, such an outlook does not always work well within the project setting. When the goal of the project team is to identify the scope and to strictly contain it within a baseline document, ongoing proposed perceived improvement in features and performance of project deliverables detracts from the scope containment effort. This continuous improvement outlook associated with understanding client requirements and product specifications may be why many Japanese companies have not been as successful in the global wireless market as they have in previous years with the more stable consumer electronics markets such as TV, DVD, and VCR. Continuous improvement of process within manufacturing as well as in project management process improvement as an ongoing activity of the sponsoring organization of the project yields significant benefits. However, "chasing the ideal project deliverable" in

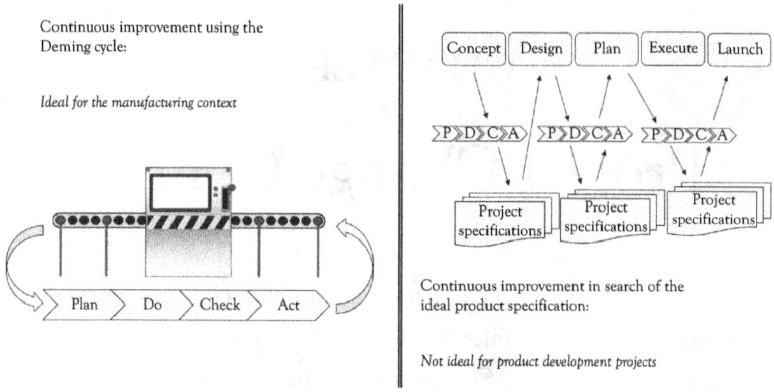

Figure 5.1 Continuous improvement: Not ideal within the product development lifecycle

the midst of an ongoing project is an ideal that feeds scope creep, budget, and schedule overruns (Figure 5.1).

It is always a struggle to lock down client requirements and specifications within an industry that is changing very rapidly and where client requirements are also fluctuate. However, having the mindset of continuous change up to the last minute of the project completion is a formula for project failure. This situation is one of the reasons why it is very important for a global project to implement a strong change control system. Not only the clients but all team members should understand that in many respects "change is an enemy."

Project Change as a Form of Waste

As in the case of manufacturing using the "Toyota Way," waste is an enemy and inventory is a form of waste. In the global project environment, specifications that are continually optimized but never fully realized in a product represent wasted effort and wasted project investment. The project manager leading the global team must ensure that all team members distributed around the globe understand the notion that *change equals cost*. Further, it should be understood that the intent of the project is to create a scope schedule and budget baseline from which all distributed teams as well as the client approves. Once approval is obtained from stakeholders, no change will be informally accepted and no changes will

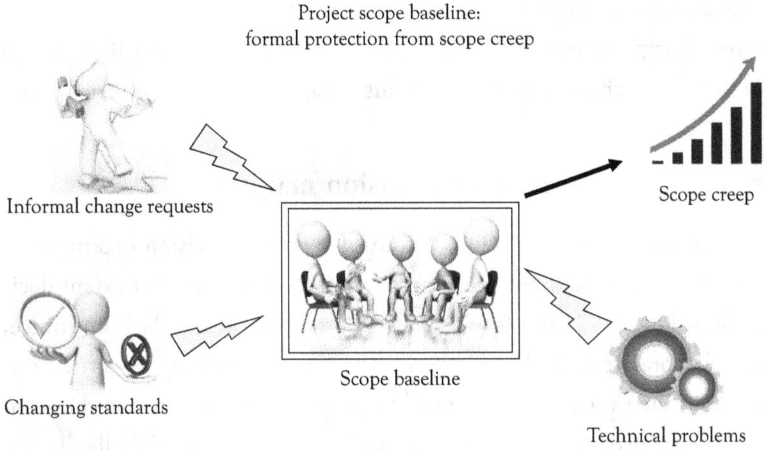

Figure 5.2 The project scope baseline

be automatically approved as well. Instead changes are requested, they are evaluated, and, if approved, they typically involve additional cost or additional budget. If they are adopted then, based on the requirements of the change, a new baseline will be agreed on and followed. Projects always suffer from scope creep regardless of the client because project teams tend to uncover additional scope and unknown items that were not originally considered as problems arise throughout the project. However, a client source of scope increase comes from informal requests to the project team (Figure 5.2).

Seemingly small requests for change in scope can cause ripple effects throughout the project it is informally accepted. There is the old saying that if "you collect enough dust eventually it becomes a mountain" illustrates the principle of the growth of informal unchecked scope change requests. The larger the team the more globally distributed the team and the greater the chance that stakeholders and representatives of the client will contact team members and make such informal requests. It is incumbent upon the project manager to make it clear that all requests must be formalized and must be presented to the Change Control Board (CCB) for evaluation. Further, the change control system supported by an enterprise wide electronic system is very useful for this purpose. In the absence of this type of sophisticated system however, every team member should be aware that when a change is proposed, it is clearly documented and submitted for consideration. Further, the global project manager must clearly communicate the expectation that no action will be taken on requested changes unless the change is approved by the global CCB.

Project Decision making

A topic that is related to change control is project decision making. The project manager leading the global team must decide to what extent decisions will be made autonomously by the project team and the home office, or collaboratively. Collaboration in decision making may be carried out between the project manager and the project team, or between the team leading the overall project at the head office together with globally distributed local teams. Further, the project manager should consider what type of decisions should best be made by locally distributed team members or at minimum what input or guidance is required from the project team's head office. The decision-making policy must be made clear and could be effectively communicated to all teams by using a PARIS or RACI chart. Such a table would identify categories of decisions such as purely local decision making that are well within the bounds of the work that has been delegated to a local team versus strategic decisions that may have a ripple effect through all project teams around the globe. Regardless of what policy is arrived at by the global project manager, it is recommended that the project manager consider some input from representatives from teams around the world.

Local Versus Global Outlook

A common problem in global project teams is that the local teams see issues arise that do not make it on the radar of the team at the head office. Therefore, priorities naturally tend to differ between the head office and globally distributed teams. Further, the sense of urgency associated with typical day-to-day project decisions may often be different. The local team may think that the head office is "out of touch," does not correctly understand the local situation, and therefore is not making the appropriate decisions at the appropriate time. There is another way to view this difference in outlook. The project team at the head office that

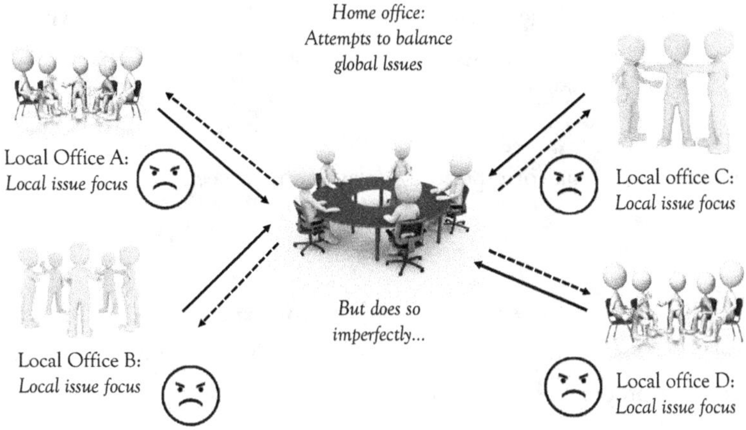

Figure 5.3 The challenge of balancing global and local issues

manages all geographically distributed teams has concerns from all teams to think about daily. Because of this, the head office project team will naturally have a difficult job of balancing priorities. In order to minimize distrust and resentment based on decision-making policy, it is essential that the project manager defines roles and responsibilities in decision making clearly and define the decision-making process. The head office project team must also be observed to use the process so that whenever a decision needs to be made, the mechanics of making decisions will operate efficiently. Another concern is ensuring that all team members are aware of the decision-making process for business and commercial issues versus purely technical issues. The two processes may need to differ in practice due to the individuals involved and the relevant expertise required (Figure 5.3).

Often technical domains and business domains are kept separate within a project so determining the decision-making flow of the process between these two is often not difficult. However, what may be difficult is understanding where to go and what process to follow to obtain a purely technical decision when the technical problem encountered is one that crosses multiple technological domains. This is one reason why the change control processes are put in place so that a cross functional multidisciplinary team may examine the proposed change in detail and determine and evaluate the implications across all technical domains. All levels of the global distributed project teams must have policies that describe how to resolve technical issues that require decisions as well as who to contact and how to do so rapidly and judiciously. Such decisions may rise to the level of the CCB. However, any time a project team member must stop what they are doing and think about it, it leads to wasted time and money along with a corresponding delay in the project.

Iterative Processes

It has been acknowledged even among low-context cultures that the overhead associated with process management within the project management and product development environment can be burdensome. This is particularly true in the case of software-intensive projects. It is for this reason that many new "light-weight" approaches to process management have evolved. These include Agile/Scrum and other iterative methods. The popularity of the new process methods has led to its incorporation within the latest edition of the PMBOK. These approaches to process tend to emphasize a strong component of personal interaction, verbal communication, and producing small pieces of functionality on a regular basis. A global project manager leading a project that interacts with team members who emphasize face-to-face communication rather than documentation may wish to consider implementing processes that are a better fit with high-context cultures (Figure 5.4) (Project Management Institute 2017).

In absence of using an iterative or agile lightweight process, another possibility is to send a project team member from the team leading the

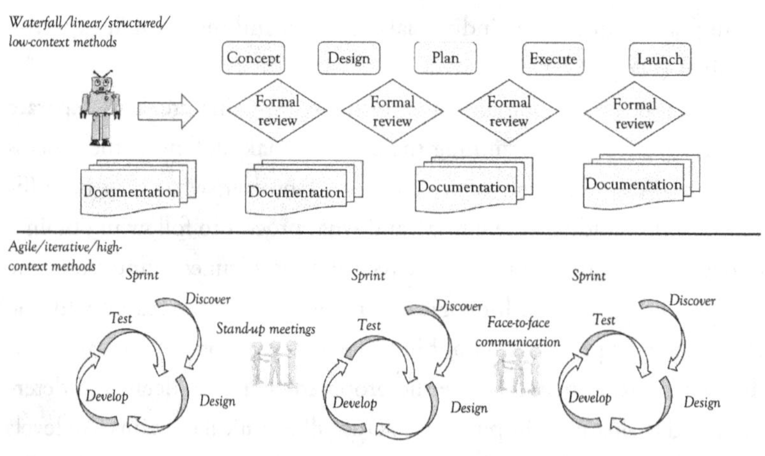

Figure 5.4 Waterfall versus iterative methods

global project to carefully document process via interviewing local team members. The interviews focus on capturing what is observed so that current processes that are employed yet undocumented may become documented. The newly created documentation provides a guiding reference so that process is followed even though the team members themselves do not fully accept the need for and importance of full documentation. The extent to which each culture can focus on doing what seems most natural will facilitate the ease of management of the global teams and make it more straightforward to produce successful outcomes.

Project Tools and Practices

Geographically distributed teams are likely to favor the use of familiar tools for communication, documentation, project management, and technical tools such as software development environments. The project manager when leading the development of the project plan includes planning for standardization of tools and methods as means for converting outputs so that project technical work products are compatible (Figure 5.5).

Beyond tool usage, this concept extends to design practices such as component tolerances, software design and documentation standards, and circuit board layouts, to name a few examples from global electronics projects. Since project deliverables are constrained by the toolsets that produce them, part of coordinating global teams by means of "standardization of outputs" will naturally lead to the establishment of tool and development environment global policies.

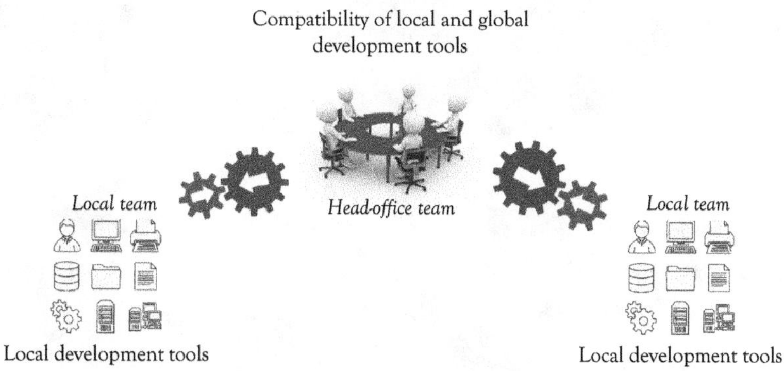

Figure 5.5 Global versus local tool decisions

CHAPTER 6
Culture and Geography

Project managers leading global projects encounter as many different cultures as there are geographies around the world. In fact, project managers may well glean information about culture, outlook on life, and shared norms and customs by gaining a better understanding and appreciation of the geography in which the culture springs. Such geographical ties to culture may be illustrated by comparing two very different cultures including the United States and Asia. The wide-open spaces of the geography of the United States plays a formative role with respect to the culture of the United States. The westward growth of the United States was led by pioneers who prided themselves in rugged individualism. The pioneers used the land they encountered to undertake European style agriculture by raising food and cash crops along with cattle. European agriculture requires that ground lie fallow after a period of years, and during the winter, work on the farm slows down. These traditions fostered the concept of "rest" after a long period of hard work as well as moving on to amply available new land when the existing land was exhausted.

Culture and Abundant Resources

The United States enjoys nearly unlimited land and natural resources and therefore the people of the United States tend to have the tendency to be unfamiliar with constraints and scarcity. There is a natural optimism and "can-do" attitude born out of the history of finding new land and opportunity, breaking new ground, and going from "rags to riches" in the process. It should therefore be no surprise to cultures outside of the United States to view Americans as overconfident, loud, and intensely focused on personal achievement. Further, the comparatively large distances between U.S. cities paired with the "DIY" or "Do it yourself" mentality tends to keep pickup trucks and large SUVs high in the list of top-selling vehicles every quarter.

The link between U.S. geography and culture is therefore tangible. The link between culture and geography may also be observed within countries and regions within large countries as well as between countries. This is especially true of large countries that have significant differences both in geography and weather associated with that geography. Consider for example the difference between the northern U.S. states and states in the southern United States. Northern states experience very long very cold winters that are often harsh. Southern U.S. states are much more temperate and have shorter and much less colder winters. It snows very little in southern U.S. states as compared to the northern states. Therefore, it is not surprising that tangible differences in cultures and behaviors are observed. It is observed that the pace of life in southern states appears to be slower for those who are from the north and this is reflected in the accent and the speech used. Those who live in the northern states traditionally use the time between the winters to prepare for the coming long cold harsh winter. Such activity is often frenetic—and those who are not native to the region may perceive significant differences in the pace of life. Locals in such regions understand that insufficient preparation could result in very high risks when winter inevitably arrives. The much more temperate year-round weather environment the southern U.S. states requires no such sense of urgency for basic survival and this is reflected in the differences between the cultures.

Japanese Geography and Culture

In contrast to the wide-open spaces of the United States, Asia, particularly Japan and South Korea, lacks the land and natural resources that the U.S. culture takes for granted. Little land is available for cultivation, particularly for European-style agriculture. The agriculture present in these countries is based on rice rather than wheat, corn, and potatoes. Rice agriculture lends itself to a collectivist approach as the work is exhausting. Groups are required to tend to flooding rice fields, planting rice, and frequently weeding it. The working of the rice field requires attention to fine detail. Further, unlike Western agriculture, which requires that the ground periodically lie fallow in order to rest and rejuvenate, rice agriculture tends to increase in production the more the ground is worked as well as the more often it is planted. Rice agriculture takes place

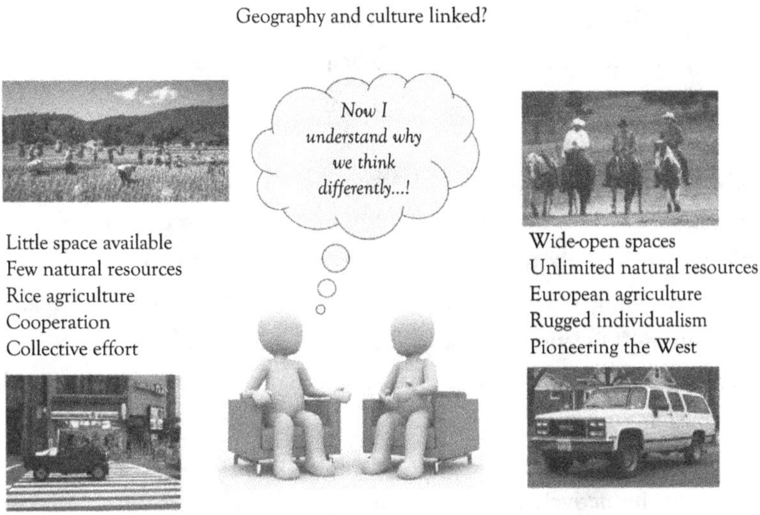

Figure 6.1 The link between culture and geography

year-round and does not necessarily follow the "plant in the spring, harvest in the fall" approach of European-based agriculture. The concept of "rest" therefore differs in perceived importance between Japanese and U.S. culture (Figure 6.1) (Gladwell 2008).

What Are the Implications?

In cases of extreme geographical differences in geographical characteristics, it should not be surprising that one culture (Asia—particularly Japan/South Korea)

- favors a collective/group effort,
- favors cooperation,
- lives within significant geographical constraints,
- perceives the need to work continuously,
- highly focused on detail, and
- has a long-term perspective.

Whereas a significantly different culture (Western countries—particularly the United States):

- favors individual efforts;
- perceives the importance of conflict in settling differences;

- unfamiliar with geographical constraints;
- perceives the concept of rest to be important; and
- has a short-term perspective.

An additional implication of the differences in geography is the overall generic worldview. A geography with significant constraints that fosters collectivism is likely to favor an inductive or "bottom-up" view of the world. The inductive view seeks to build up a "big picture" from many observations. Direction gradually emerges over time. The Asian consensus process is in alignment with the deductive approach to thinking. Instead of conceiving of a strategy at the highest levels of the organization and pushing it downward to the rank and file employees, strategy tends to bubble up inductively as the consensus position emerges. On the other hand, the lack of constraints associated with nearly unlimited geographical resources supports a top-down outlook where "bets are placed" and risks are willingly taken. This is a top-down or deductive approach and is a less cautious worldview. It could be said that this is a natural result of having the "safety net" of wide-open spaces and significant resources. The top-down and bottom-up approaches are likely to clash and lead to significant differences in risk appetite. A global project manager may not be able to change the outlook of stakeholders, but at minimum, project stakeholders may better understand and appreciate the differences in perspectives as well as the ultimate source from which it springs.

Cultural Dimensions

The theory regarding high versus low context as well as differences that are linked to geographical context is a good beginning step for understanding culture. However, it is only one of the many approaches for trying to understand the differences between cultures around the world. An important lens for understanding culture is the theory of cultural dimensions. There are a series of cultural dimensions developed by academics and business professionals over the last forty years. Cultural dimensions are an attempt to understand better exactly how and why different people from different geographical regions are different as well as in what way they are different. Are there typical patterns that exist and if so what are they? There are two important historical cultural dimensions: Hofstede's cultural dimensions and the cultural dimensions developed by Trompenaars. Hofstede was a human resources professional from IBM who studied IBM operations around the world. He used this ready-made set of data to try and understand what differences might exist in geographically distributed IBM operations. This is a practical study that provided significant information. However, some scholars have critiqued Hofstede's dimensions because they lack adequate theoretical grounding. Trompenaars is another scholar who studied dimensions of national culture. Trompenaars was said to have begun his focus on cultural dimensions from a background in anthropology. Trompenaars' cultural dimensions are therefore thought of as being more grounded in scholarly theory. In practice, however, both Hofstede and Trompenaars' analyses of national cultures may seem similar in content to project managers. Although the cultural dimensions may not be definitive summaries of how and why people are different around the world, they do provide some clues for project managers to help them understand in what way might they shift their expectations or perhaps adjust their approach when doing business in different geographical regions.

Hofstede's Dimensions

Power Distance

Hofstede developed six different dimensions in which cultures are measured. These dimensions are characteristics said to exist in different cultures. The dimensions are designed in such a way that the degree to which each of these characteristics differ is used to assess in what respect one culture may differ from another. The first Hofstede dimension is known as *power distance*. Power distance is a measure of the degree to which egalitarian culture might be favored versus a hierarchical structure. Sometimes differences in power distances are observed within a single culture. For example, a very high power distance is likely to exist in a traditional company such as an automobile manufacturer. By contrast, however, a very low power distance in a startup company is typical of what might be found in Silicon Valley. Power distance therefore is a measure of how particular culture may be egalitarian or hierarchical or said another way, prefer organic and loosely managed organizations as opposed to highly structured mechanistic, functional organizations. It is important for project managers understand power distance characteristics within countries in which the project is doing business. If, for example, there is a great difference in power distance between the home country of the project team and the country in which a geographically distant team would operate, this difference may provide insights regarding how the team might want to organize the project.

Individualism

Individualism is the second Hofstede cultural dimension. Many Western countries, especially the United States, are highly individualistic in outlook. Recall, for example, the analysis of the United States from the perspective of geography. Individuals in the formative years of the United States were known to be pioneers. They were very self-sufficient and individuals from the United States who often perceive themselves to be this way even today. Because of this, we see that projects that are managed out of the United States may tend to favor a more individualistic approach. This may include recognizing individual versus group achievement, taking risk, thinking of individual needs and responsibilities versus those assigned to others. The contrast to individualism is collectivism. Many cultures are known to be collectivist in their outlook. Many Asian cultures fall into this category. For example, the People's Republic of China, Japanese culture, and the countries that formed parts of the former Soviet Union are categorized by Hofstede as highly collectivist in outlook. The emphasis in the collectivist culture is to favor the group over the individual. An example of a possible problem that a project manager might experience when coming from an individualistic perspective in dealing with the collectivist perspective is in the compensation scheme. Is the project team going to, for example, incentivize individuals for their performance? Or, is the team going to emphasize group incentives? If the project team emphasizes individual rewards to the exclusion of collective compensation schemes and the project is operating in a culture that according to Hofstede's research is assessed as being highly collectivist in outlook, the project may encounter morale problems as well as a serious mismatch of expectations.

Masculinity

The next Hofstede dimension is *masculinity.* A masculine versus feminine culture is a contrast between power versus nurture. It is also the degree to which gender roles are similar or different. One notable example of differences in gender roles is Japan versus the People's Republic of China. In Japan it is much less common for females to assume management roles, especially top management roles. However, in the People's Republic of China it is very common to see female CEOs alongside male CEOs with perhaps similar numbers observed between them. Fewer differences are observed in gender roles in the People's Republic of China than that observed in Japan. This corresponds to different scores in Hofstede's masculinity dimension. Masculinity scores also provide the implication that a very low masculinity score signifies that nurture is more important than aggressiveness and expression of power.

Uncertainty Avoidance

The fourth dimension identified by Hofstede is *uncertainty avoidance.* Uncertainty avoidance is described in different ways in different cultures around the world. For example, uncertainty avoidance may be evident in the body of laws employed within a country. It may be perceived, for example, that reliance on tradition and previous rulings may introduce an element of risk in terms of controls over behavior in society and court rulings. For this reason, cultures that emphasize on uncertainty avoidance may to resolve this by favoring the codification of laws. Therefore it is observed that in the United States, there is less emphasis on avoiding uncertainty, which translates into higher risk appetite. Correspondingly, there is a long-term tradition of less codification within the U.S. legal environment that has as its origin in the Anglo-Saxon tradition of common law. On the other hand, it is observed in France and Spain (and to a certain extent Germany) that more emphasis is placed on the codification of laws. The general indication here is that these cultures tend to favor the reduction of uncertainty. There is evidence that some cultural dimensions may change over time. As an example, the United States is observed to be moving toward increasing codification of laws and avoidance of uncertainty, particularly within the world of finance. For example, from within the legal environment of the financial world, the Sarbanes-Oxley as well as the Dodd Frank rules have emerged over the last 20 years. These legal codes seek to put in black-and-white areas that may have previously required the application of judgment.

Long-Term Orientation

Hofstede also identifies *long-term orientation* as an important dimension of culture. Cultures that have a high long-term orientation score tend to worry less about the next day, the next week, or the next quarter and instead look ahead for generations. Asian countries tend to score highly in long-term orientation. Though the Asian stock market's emphasis on returns is changing gradually due to its participation in the global capital markets, traditionally Asian public companies have emphasized low returns and long-term security. This contrasts with the emphasis on quick stock market gains and high quarterly returns favored by many Western cultures. Western companies tend to have a laser focus on earnings reports and the stock price. The short-term orientation is also a characteristic of startup companies that seek to achieve some immediate targets, be acquired, and taken public so that the initial shareholders may "cash out." Clear differences in orientation between cultures are therefore observed between the long-term and the short-term.

Restraint Versus Indulgence

The sixth cultural dimension involves research restraint versus indulgence. In this dimension, some cultures consider happiness to always be a good thing, whereas some cultures may feel that it is preferred to be more restrained. In fact, some cultures may consider too much happiness to be unnecessary at best, and perhaps even a negative experience. A person within a culture of restraint, for example, may not particularly "enjoy" work as it is considered important in the classical Western tradition. Work in this view is not supposed to be "enjoyed." A culture of restraint tends to produce demonstrations of strong personal discipline. As a classical example of this, it is often observed in Japanese companies—as well as some companies in other countries who have a culture of restraint—will avoid taking advantage of company policies that allow for traveling by business class or staying in a better class of hotels. The idea here is that even though the policy allows for some personal comforts while traveling, it is considered important to exercise personal restraint within the culture and forgo activities signal indulgence in any way. This thinking may be a reason for the very long hours put in by workers in most Japanese companies. It is not uncommon to work 12- to 14-hour days, as leaving work at a time that most Westerners would have considered reasonable, would be seen to be an act of indulgence. Perhaps it is this work ethic and personal discipline that substitutes for the lack of process discipline observed in high-context cultures.

Western companies may have different views on restraint versus indulgence that are based on company norms rather than being exclusively linked to national cultural dimensions. This is an issue to consider in project management, but it is also revealed itself in ongoing operations. For example, consider the Daimler Chrysler merger of several years ago. There was a significant mismatch between restraint and indulgence between the two companies, which often led to serious disagreements. It is this basic difference in culture between the two companies that led to a breakdown and termination of the merger (Figure 6.2) (Hofstede 2003).

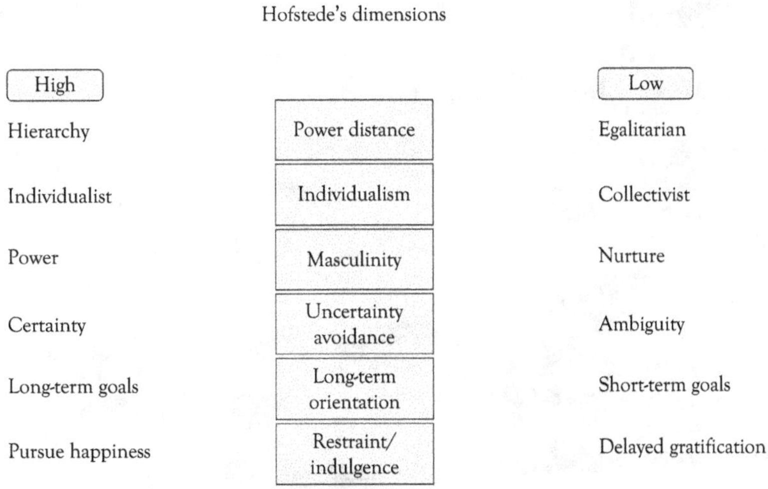

Figure 6.2 Hofstede's cultural dimensions

How Would a Project Team Use Hofstede?

The basic idea behind the use of cultural dimensions is to increase the understanding of different cultures by comparing similarities and differences between the scores of cultural dimensions measured in each country. Such differences may also suggest to a project team what to expect from a different cultural setting as well as what behaviors the team may consider modifying. As an example, the project team in the home country may score low on the "uncertainty avoidance" dimension, whereas the client in a different country and cultural setting may score high. If this is the case, the project team may consider developing and communicating clear policies, procedures, and rules for the purpose of minimizing ambiguity. Further, the team may consider that the client may demand fixed schedule baselines and be very unhappy with schedules that change frequently. Figure 6.3 illustrates a country comparison of Hofstede dimensions that are typical of what a project team might use as part of the cultural analysis and preparation.

Trompenaars

Although Trompenaars cultural dimensions were developed using a different research methodology, they do appear to have several similarities to Hofstede's dimensions. Because of this, project managers often find

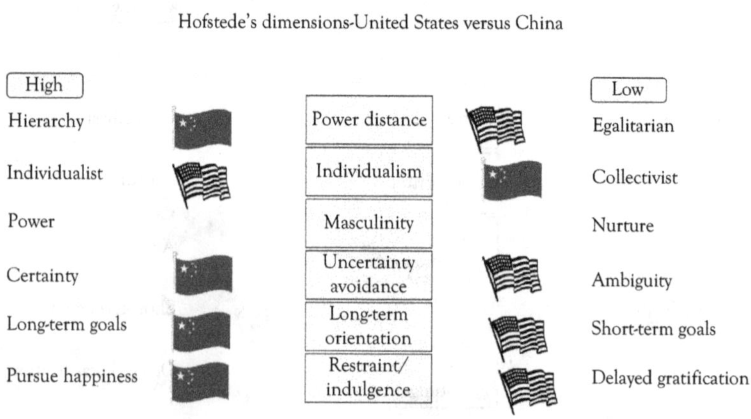

Figure 6.3 Application of Hofstede's dimensions

both Hofstede and Trompenaars informative in that they both provide important clues about how cultures in different parts of the world tend to behave. Both dimensional frameworks together provide a more holistic set of observations that together aid in better understanding global cultures.

Universalism Versus Particularism

The first cultural dimension developed by Trompenaars is *universalism* versus *particularism*. This dimension bears strong resemblance to the "high-context/low-context" cultural categorization. For example, universalism versus particularism seeks to understand if individuals exhibit consistent behavior or if their behavior tends to change depending on the context. In many Asian countries, the consideration of context is observed to be essential. It is natural to assume in a high-context culture that particularism will be the overriding cultural dimension.

Individualism Versus Collectivism

Like Hofstede, Trompenaars includes a dimension identifying the degree of individualism versus collectivism within a culture. Trompenaars concept appears to be the same as that described by Hofstede. The sense of both frameworks is that cultures tend to vary depending on the degree to which the individual versus the group is favored in rewards and recognition. A collectivist culture will view the group to which one belongs as being more important than any one individual within the group and policies will naturally reflect this.

Neutral Versus Affective

The next dimension developed by Trompenaars is the neutral versus affective dimension. This dimension describes the degree to which a culture finds it acceptable to openly display or hide emotions. For many cultures, the acceptability of emotional display will depend upon the context. There is a saying in Japan that "the eagle never shows his claws" and in high-context cultures showing emotion in a leadership position may be considered at times to be a sign of immaturity. Culture that has more of an effective outlook may consider showing emotion a good thing. In fact, stakeholders in some cultures may bond better with a leader who expresses emotion and this behavior may be perceived in some cultures as being charismatic. Another example from Japan regarding expressing emotions versus neutrality is in the annual policy meeting. The annual policy meeting outlines the strategy and goals that the company is going to achieve for the next year and this is something that is done at the beginning of every year to kick off the fiscal year (Figure 6.4) (Smith, Dugan, and Trompenaars 1996).

A Westerner would find a policy meeting in Japan completely devoid of emotion. The focus is on sales goals, inventory levels, product details, and other business details one would not expect to hear from a highly charismatic leader. A Westerner, or an individual from a culture who is familiar with a leader expressing emotion, may expect that the policy meeting may be formatted more like an annual kick-off meeting. In this type of meeting, the leader plays the role of the cheerleader expressing a highly positive emotion. The intent of a Western-style kick-off meeting would be not only to express the goals of the company but to provide insights as to why the mission of the company is important, why the contribution of every individual is important, and why it is a good thing to be a part of the company. Such an emotional appeal is made so that team members understand that the company is something larger than all

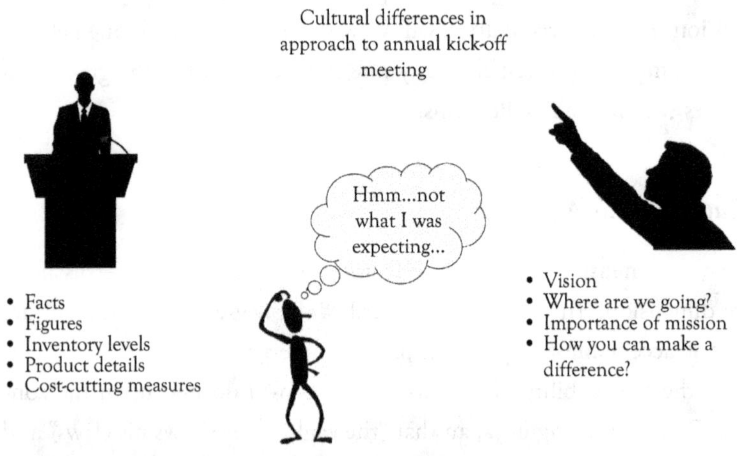

Figure 6.4 Expectations mismatch between cultures

the individuals. It explains the "why" behind the company's mission as opposed to "what." Although this style of speaking is appreciated in many cultures, the emotional appeal is not something that is expected by stakeholders in a culture that does not favor emotional expressions from the leaders. Within a global project, team leaders may encounter a mismatch of expectations between the leader and his followers in cultures that have neutral versus affective emotional expression. This is an important leadership issue for project managers to consider depending on what cultures they may encounter in global projects.

Achievement and Ascription

Trompenaars follows the neutral and effective with *achievement* and *ascription*. Achievement and ascription lie on a spectrum from which an individual considers it important to *be something* (ascription) rather than to *do something* (achievement). Is success viewed as something gained from what a person does or does success flow from what that person is? In some ways, achievement versus ascription may be related to favoring a group versus the individual. For example, in high context and collectivist cultures "what one is" is often a function of group affiliation and thereby observed to be more important than what one does as an individual. When seen in this perspective, ascription, achievement, collectivist, individualistic, and high and low context overlap in many ways as described.

Specific Versus Diffuse

Trompenaars follows achievement and ascription with the dimensions of *specific* and *diffuse*. This dimension measures the extent to which the world is viewed as linked together or considered to be separate. Once again, this is a dimension that appears to offer similarities with collectivism and individualism although the idea extends beyond groups and individuals to reality itself. Another way to think of specific versus diffuse is mechanistic versus organic. A mechanistic philosophical viewpoint suggests that all complex systems may be broken down and analyzed in terms of its components. An organic perspective is consistent with the view that the complexity associated with people, organizations, and life in general is best understood holistically. Clearly cultures that are more focused on the group rather than the individual may find that the diffuse end of the spectrum to be more favorable. This viewpoint may be preferred over the mechanistic point of view on life associated with Western cultures. Many Western cultures therefore will exhibit a tendency to view the world on the specific rather than the diffuse portion of this dimension.

Sequential Versus Synchronic

The final two dimensions from Trompenaars involve how time is handled. The *sequential* point of view on time is that activities must be carried out one at a time. The *synchronic* view assumes that it is perfectly acceptable to multitask and attempt to do many different things at once. Another way to understand the difference between sequential versus synchronic is to consider to what degree the environment is perceived to control individuals, or do individuals manage the environment? Project managers are likely to experience that the sequential step-by-step approach to time corresponds well to a low-context mechanistic approach along with a high focus on managing a process.

Inner Versus Outer Directed

Inner versus outer directed is a measure of the degree to which individuals consider that they control their own destiny or do not. A culture associated with rugged individualism or perhaps in the United States where there is a traditional belief that anyone has the potential to be highly successful clearly illustrates an inner-directed viewpoint. In this viewpoint, things do not just happen on their own—but rather—individuals "make things happen." In some cultures, the phrase "God willing" may appear in conversations, which is an indication of an outer directed focus. Project managers should carefully assess leaders to determine their level of inner directedness versus and outer-directed viewpoint. Global projects are likely to benefit from leaders who do have the sense that they can control their own destiny using their skills and their own management efforts. This outlook is to be preferred over leaders who reflect the idea that that regardless of their individual efforts things are likely to happen

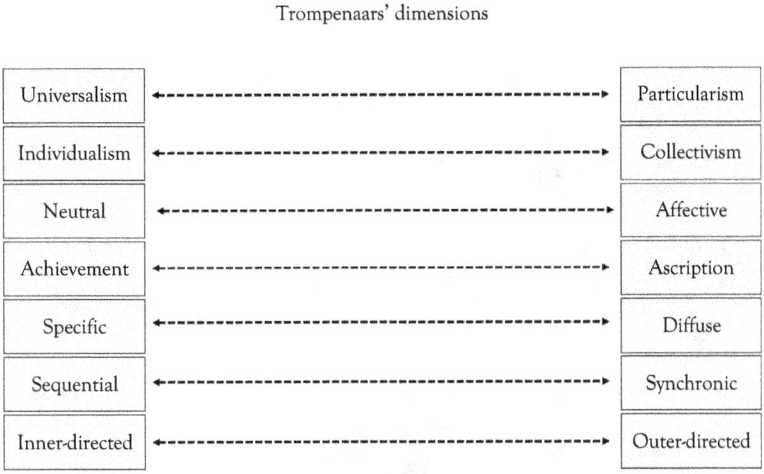

Figure 6.5 Trompenaar's cultural framework

that are not necessarily within their control. Another way to think of this is whether a leader has an inner or outer locus of control.

Consistent with the saying, "leaders do the right thing, but managers do things right," a successful leader will likely have a strong internal locus of control whereas a manager may need clear and explicit direction to satisfy the outer locus of control. Trompenaars' dimensions are summarized in Figure 6.5.

How Would a Project Team Use Trompenaars?

Although the dimensions are different from that of Hofstede, a project team would employ the dimensions in the same way as that of Hofstede, particularly within areas that the project team would consider to be important. If the project team from the home country is associated with a highly individualist culture, it may be of concern to know the degree to which the client country is individualistic versus collectivist in outlook. A comparison of two countries on this dimension is given in Figure 6.6.

The individual/collectivist dimensional example is but one of many. A quick scan of all of Trompenaars' dimensions is likely to be useful in a brainstorming session to assess what dimensions that are not well understood are likely to cause problems within a project.

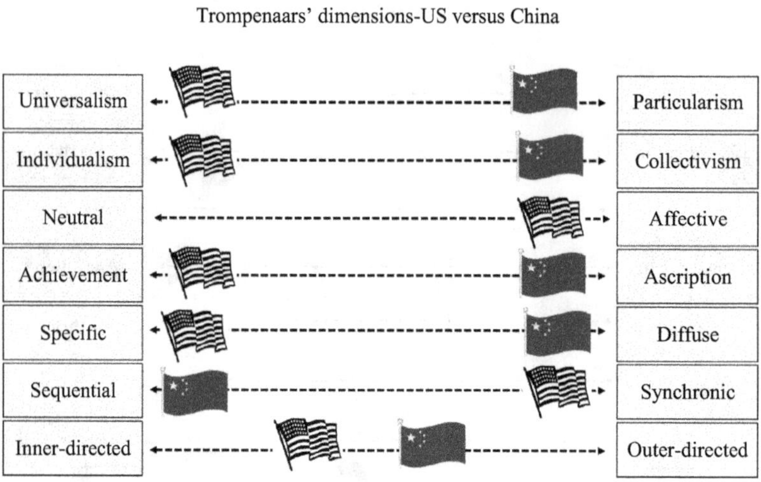

***Figure 6.6** Application of Trompenaar's framework*

The World Values Survey

The World Values Survey takes a different approach from both Hofstede and Trompenaars. Instead of identifying unique cultural dimensions, the World Values Survey seeks to understand how people from different regions of the world differ by collecting a significant amount of varied information in the survey form. The World Values Survey does attempt to categorize cultures based upon the findings from different iterations of their surveys that have gone out to nearly every country in the world, but is the detailed data collected from the surveys themselves that prove useful to project managers. As an example of how a global project manager might use the World Values Survey, the project manager could go to the World Values Survey website and download raw survey data for analysis. Another approach would be to compare results from two different countries to understand the differences in how each country responded to many of the survey questions. Survey questions provide deep insights into what people think in different parts of the world and a project manager can compare survey results from one country to another with ease. Upon seeing the differences in approaches of two different countries and cultures, project managers could adjust, for example, how the project is organized or how it intends to communicate to stakeholders within the culture in which the project will be operating (Figure 6.7) (World Values Survey 2019).

Culture map derived from world values survey

(Inglehart-Welzel 2008)

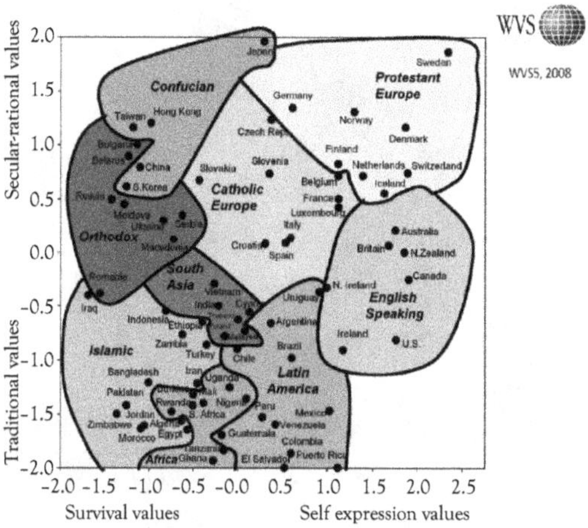

Figure 6.7 World Values Survey culture map

How Would a Project Team Use the World Values Survey?

The World Values Survey is a highly detailed instrument administered in countries around the world. Unlike Hofstede and Trompenaars, the survey results do not equate to a series of dimensions. Although the data are richer than the already distilled data from cultural dimensions, the project team may need to perform analysis to compare responses on specific survey questions to obtain a better understanding about differences between their cultures and others with which the team will be working. An example of a comparison of survey responses on the World Values Survey is given in Figure 6.8. This is one comparison among hundreds of questions in the survey. The selected questions in this example provide evidence of responses consistent with a high-context culture, and a general collectivist outlook in terms of cultural dimensions.

Why Not Compare Them All?

It is observed that similarities, differences, and overlaps exist between Hofstede, Trompenaars, and the World Values Survey. What is a global project team to make of it? Perhaps the best approach is to seek to obtain a holistic view by comparing cultures using Hofstede, Trompenaars, and specific elements of the World Values Survey. When the data is collected, as in this example in Figure 6.9, the bigger picture begins to emerge.

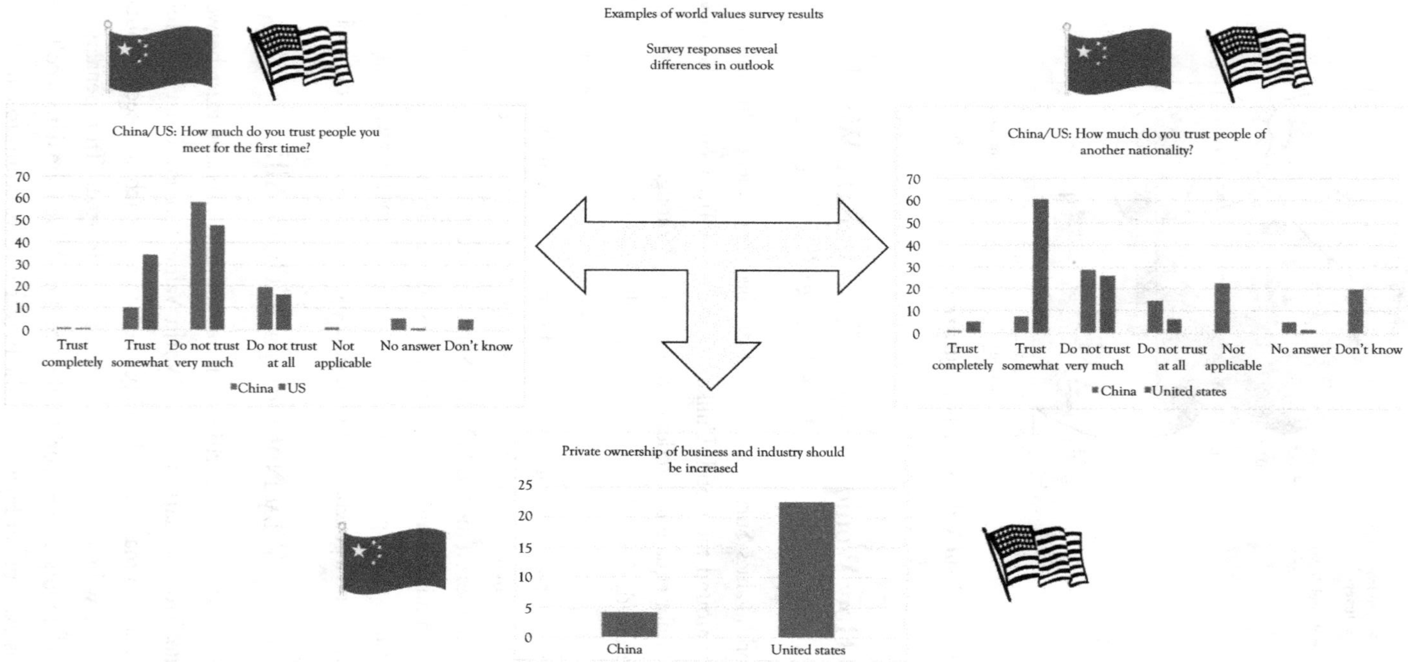

Figure 6.8 ***World Values Survey response comparison***

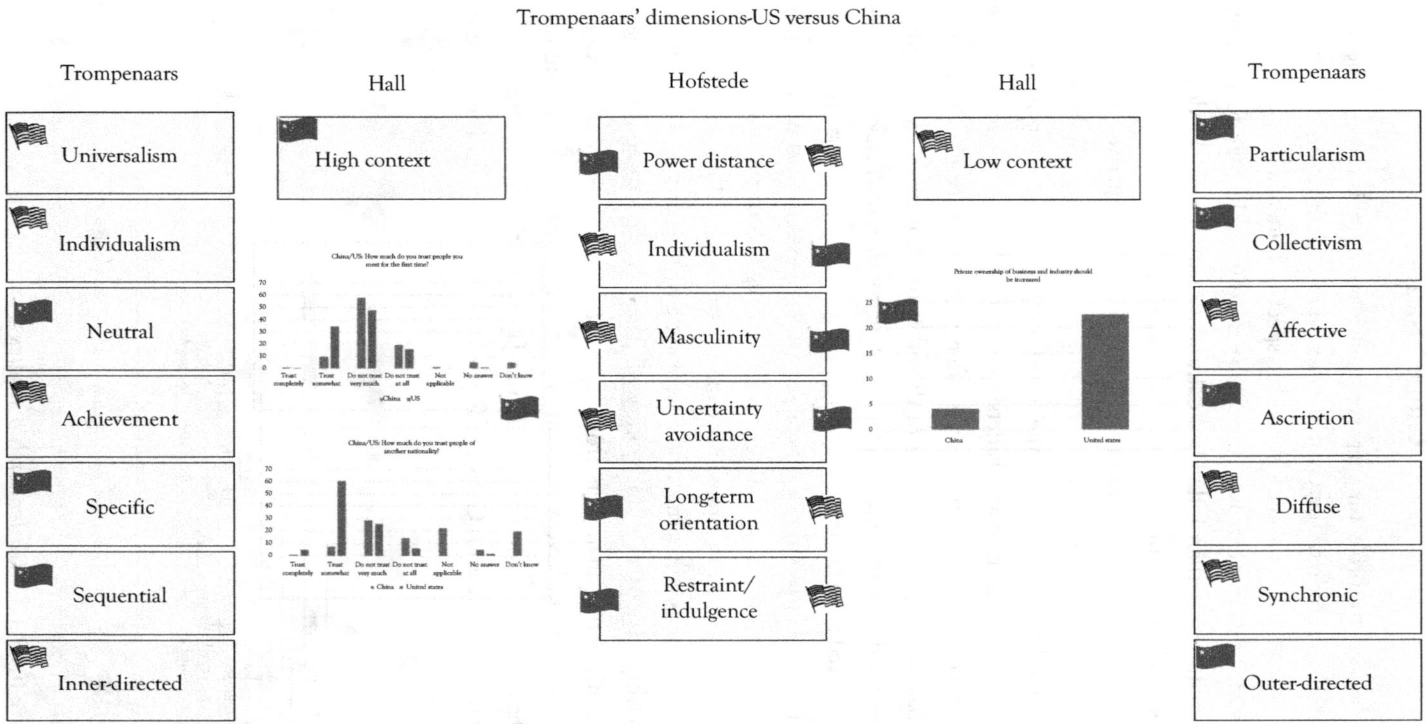
Trompenaars' dimensions-US versus China
Trompenaars
Universalism
Individualism
Neutral
Achievement
Specific
Sequential
Inner-directed
Hall
High context
China/US: How much do you trust people you meet for the first time?
China/US: How much do you trust people of another nationality?
Hofstede
Power distance
Individualism
Masculinity
Uncertainty avoidance
Long-term orientation
Restraint/ indulgence
Hall
Low context
Private ownership of business and industry should be increased
China
United states
Trompenaars
Particularism
Collectivism
Affective
Ascription
Diffuse
Synchronic
Outer-directed

Figure 6.9 Applying multiple culture frameworks

The Globe Studies

Another way for project managers to consider culture is through the lens of the Globe studies. The Globe studies were undertaken to understand the expectation of stakeholders with respect to leadership styles. Unlike Hofstede and Trompenaars, the Globe study is exclusively focused on leadership rather than individual cultural dimensions. Globe does identify several dimensions including autonomous leadership, charismatic value-based leadership, humane leadership, participative leadership, self-protective leadership, and team-oriented leadership. Globe seeks to understand which regions of the world tend to favor a given leadership style. For example, humane leadership, which is defined as being sensitive and concerned about humanity, is often preferred in Anglo, Asian, and sub-Saharan African clusters. On the other hand, team-oriented leadership—the degree to which leaders are collaborative with stakeholders—are observed to be favored in some regions but less so in others. The Globe studies could be useful in a general sense to understand what expectations may exist in leaders operating in different regions of the world. However, it is important to remember that it is not generally a good idea to think of a culture in terms of the stereotype with respect to what type of leadership may or may not work well. There are also some cases where companies bring in leaders from different cultures specifically because they are likely to have a different approach that may play a strong role in shaking up the company. Nissan in Japan did this for example when they brought in Carlos Ghosn of Renault. Ghosn is a leader immersed in

GLOBE leadership studies

GLOBE dimensions	Characteristics	Regional preferences
Autonomous leadership	Individualist	Eastern European
Charismatic/value-based leadership	Visionary	Anglo, Asian, Latin American
Humane leadership	Tolerant	Anglo, Asian, Sub-Saharan
Participative leadership	Listening	Wide variation outside Latin America and Middle-East
Self-protective leadership	Procedural	Wide variation
Team-oriented leadership	Collaborative	Anglo, Asian, Latin American

Different regions express preferences for different forms of leadership

Figure 6.10 GLOBE leadership studies

European culture and took the reins of the Japanese company steeped in a different leadership tradition. How useful are the Globe studies for global project managers? While the Globe study may provide general indicators about leadership preferences in different geographical regions, in practice, changing leadership styles according to general preferences that are somewhat lacking in specificity is likely to prove difficult (Figure 6.10) (House et al. 2004).

CHAPTER 7

Additional Leadership Considerations

The Globe studies may be useful to a degree, but they do not include all leadership issues that a project manager is likely to encounter in the global environment. One classic example of this is the day-to-day concern of scheduling work and overtime. For example, a project manager working in Japan need not request from employees that they work overtime. It is in the national culture of Japan to work overtime. It is not uncommon for most Japanese employees to work 60–80 hours per week. Often Japanese employees will catch the train in the morning and arrive at work at 8:30 a.m. and may leave work sometime between 10:00 p.m. and midnight. Although this is a grueling work–life balance, it is consistent with a country whose geography offers little in terms of natural resources and thereby relies on the labor of its citizens to survive. Also, such work practices are consistent with a culture of self-discipline or "restraint versus indulgence." A project manager will find exactly the opposite of this situation when dealing with stakeholders in Europe and particularly within Germany. In this culture, overtime must not only be requested, but it must be negotiated (Figure 7.1).

Further when a project manager requests the supplier or other stakeholders to work overtime, the initial reaction is that some mistake must have been made on the part of the management. The reason for this thinking is that if management had planned out the work more carefully, there would be no need for employees to work overtime. Therefore why should employees immediately respond to such a request to correct for problems caused by the management? Global project managers are likely to encounter completely different mindsets when leading project stakeholders in different regions. Leadership issues benefit from studying the labor environment in advance while obtaining high-level guidance

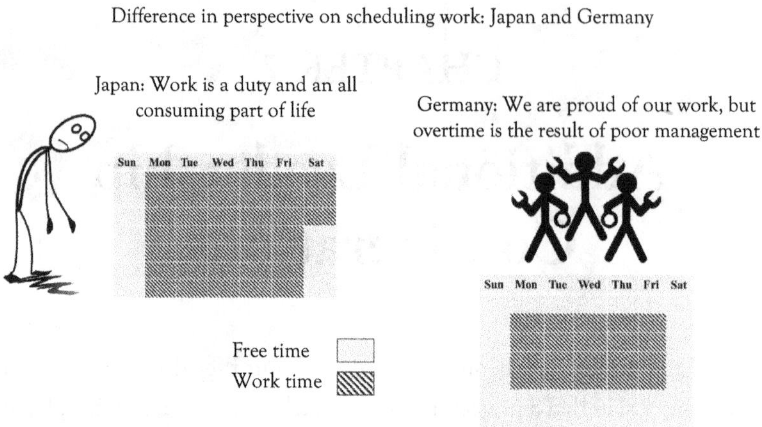

Difference in perspective on scheduling work: Japan and Germany
Japan: Work is a duty and an all consuming part of life
Sun Mon Tue Wed Thu Fri Sat
Germany: We are proud of our work, but overtime is the result of poor management
Sun Mon Tue Wed Thu Fri Sat
Free time
Work time

Figure 7.1 Culture and work scheduling perspective

from the Globe studies, Hofstede, Trompenaars, and finally, the World Values Survey.

Power and Influence in Global Projects

Regardless of leadership style deemed to be important in managing global team members and engaging with stakeholders, it is important to consider the desired outcome. A global project manager must consider what it is that is being attempted to achieve and then, based on these goals, consider how best to achieve it when interacting with global stakeholders. As the general findings of the Globe studies indicate, some cultures do not prefer the direct approach, they instead prefer direction that is far more subtle and nuanced. In contrast to this, some cultures may prefer a very direct approach and will feel lost if the leader does not take command and issue orders. Using the guidance from Globe, Hofstede, and Trompenaars, carefully consider what forms of power best fit within the context. Furthermore, for team members who do not respond well to the direct approach, envision what forms of influence may work equally well. In all cases global project managers should think of power in terms of the power and influence budget. A project manager can storm into a room and issue commands in a very direct and definitive way using emotion and an explosive expression of power and influence. However, once this is done, it may be difficult to engage in that behavior repeatedly and obtain

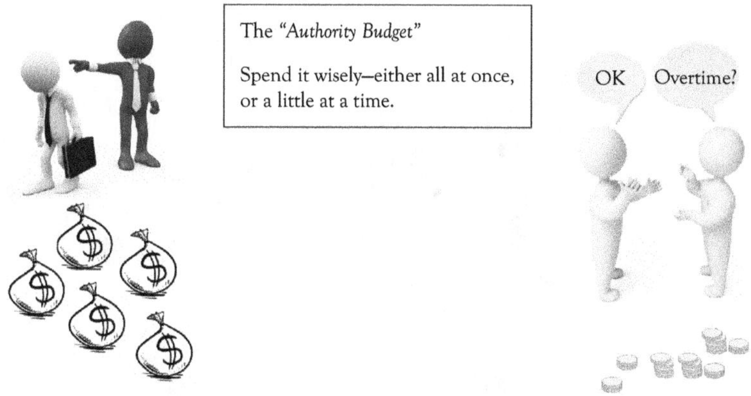

Figure 7.2 The authority budget

the same results. Instead of spending all power and influence at once, perhaps it is better to mete out power and influence bit by bit over time, thereby maintaining a power and influence budget as is employed over time (Figure 7.2).

Pull Versus Push in Project Leadership

A further consideration for global project managers is that project managers typically lack formal, legitimate power and therefore tend to manage projects by focusing on influence rather than expressions of power. There is an old saying that "you can't push on a string." Likewise, project managers encourage others to carry out the work of the project rather than issue orders. Rather than directing, the project manager uses influence in a "pull" versus "push" manner by pointing out the benefits associated with working together with the project team. What motivates different cultures around the world will naturally vary. However, from an influence perspective, identifying both individual as well as group-based benefits of working with the team, being associated with the team, and achieving success can be a very effective approach to influence.

CHAPTER 8
Practical Matters

Culture is but one facet of global project management. Culture is intangible and perhaps more theoretical than the practical day-to-day issue that the project manager will face. Everything that a project team does in the course of executing the project will involve practical differences that may well lead teams to struggle. It is useful for project managers to remember that when it comes to daily life, there is no single way of doing things that should be considered "the right way." Flexibility is always recommended when encountering and working with local norms. The saying "when in Rome, do as the Romans do" was quoted for a reason, and the reason is that fitting in to the extent possible in following local norms and customs is appreciated and can make the business of the project run much more smoothly.

Food and Culture

One of those important items that project managers and team members will encounter is food. Project stakeholders must eat to live, but what is eaten as a part of the daily diet routine differs considerably from region to region. Project team members working in different parts of the world will have to expect that the favorite local food from their home country may not always be available. Instead of hamburgers, project managers and team members are likely to encounter raw fish, unfamiliar meats and vegetables, spices, and unusual flavors (Figure 8.1).

It goes a long way with global stakeholders if time is taken to appreciate the food that is presented and at least try the food and show appreciation. Regardless of the food presented, remember that all life comes from DNA, and seek to live with unfamiliar foods if possible. Another consideration involving food is not the "what" but the "how." It is common in Western countries to use the knife and fork to eat. The use of the knife and fork, however, may differ between Western countries, particularly

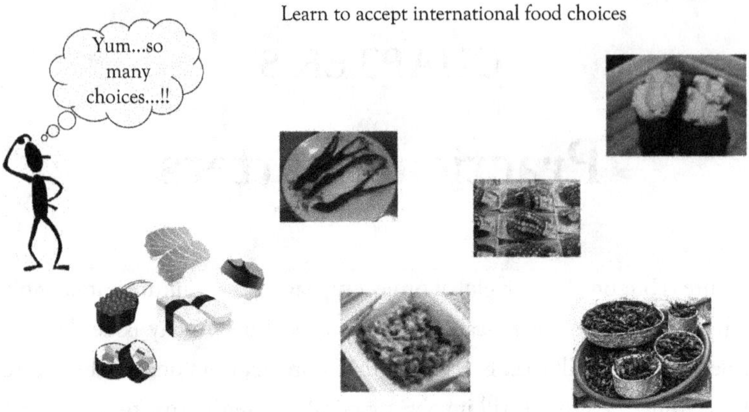

Learn to accept international food choices
Yum...so many choices...!!

Figure 8.1 Culture differences and food

between the United States and Europe. Further, the number of forks, knives, and spoons used in serving a meal is likely to differ based on the level of formality of the meal. When, for example, a project manager is requested to go to dinner with a senior executive in Europe, learning which knife, fork, and spoon to use (along with "how to use them") is important (Figure 8.2).

Asian countries are well known for the use of chopsticks for eating. Practice is recommended for new chopstick users. When attempting to use chopsticks for the first time, avoid holding them close to the tip. Also, watch for "chopstick creep"—the tendency for sauces to crawl up the chopsticks and get on the hands. It is important as well to keep in

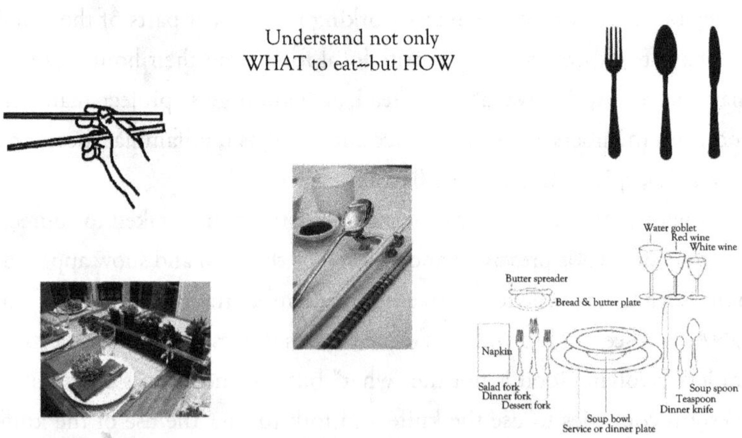

Figure 8.2 Pay attention to "how" to eat in different cultural settings

mind that even though chopsticks are presented at most meals, not all foods will be eaten that way. Soup—except for the noodles and other solid components—is usually eaten with a large ladle-like spoon. Using such a spoon may make a loud "sipping noise" when using it, but it is accepted in most Asian settings and not considered impolite as it is in the West. Finally, keep in mind that not all meals in Asia will be eaten at a table. Some meals are served on the floor such as on Tatami mats in Japan.

Food and Religious Observances

Not everyone is able to share different food practices due to religious as well as health reasons. Some cultures eat beef but not pork and vice versa. Some cultures will consume only certain types of seafood. In addition to religious cultures, some team members may be vegetarian, vegan, or have specific food allergies. If project team members can enjoy local foods, so much the better. On the other hand, if some stakeholders are not able to partake in certain foods because of certain cultural, religious, or health restrictions, this is something that should be clearly noted and respected. Nothing conveys respect more than arranging for meals that is consistent with stakeholder observances or restrictions. Such meals that are arranged by project managers may need to consider requirements for halal or kosher, stipulation against alcohol and different types of meat such as pork, beef, and various types of shellfish (Figure 8.3).

Also recall that the specific type of food may be only one part of the equation. Another issue is considering the focus on how the food

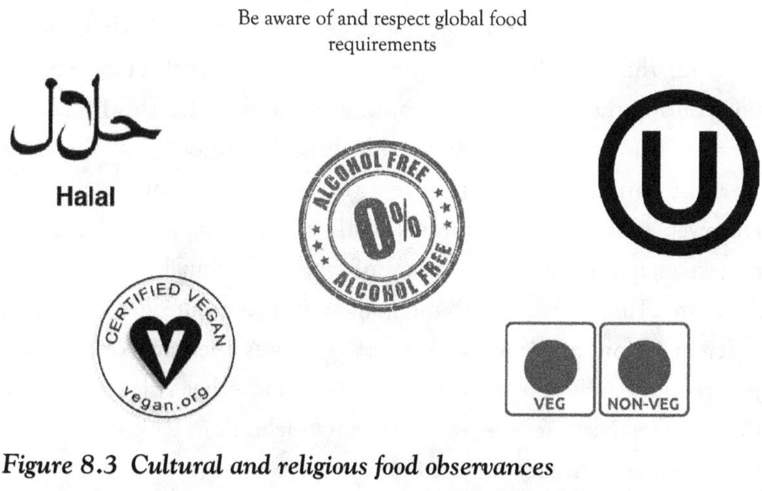

Figure 8.3 Cultural and religious food observances

is prepared. This requires some research up front, but in the context of a global project, it is a factor that must be considered especially among high-power/high-interest project stakeholders.

Holidays

Global project managers making plans and schedules must be aware that holidays around the world will vary considerably. Consider the difference between holidays in the United States and Europe. It is often said that there are two seasons in northern Europe: fall and winter. When August arrives, it is considered in Europe to be an ideal time to take a vacation. Project managers would do well to avoid scheduling important business with European clients around the August timeframe. Europe is not the only region that has holidays and holiday traditions different for many parts of the West. For example, Japanese companies typically observe something known as the "Golden Week." Golden Week occurs twice a year—once in the spring and once in the fall. Recall that Japanese culture is highly collectivist in outlook, so it is therefore unsurprising that most of the nation tends to go on vacation at the same time during these weeks. Golden week is useful for companies because factories can be shut down for maintenance as well as to obtain significant cost savings by scheduling all vacations at the same time. Also, the strong work ethic of Japanese employees suggests that unless the workplace is completely closed, there is no feasible way to take a complete vacation. Therefore, the Golden Week holidays allow for this. In Western countries, the idea of synchronizing vacations during the Golden Week could seem intolerable. This is because Western countries are more individualistic in outlook and therefore everyone naturally expects to take a vacation on their own schedules. However, synchronized vacations work well in Japanese culture and project managers should be aware of what the annual Golden Week dates are. The annual New Year holiday is also a date that differs in different regions of the world. Western countries celebrate New Year on January 1 of each year. However, in China and other Asian countries, the Chinese New Year is an important celebration. This celebration takes place in February (Figure 8.4).

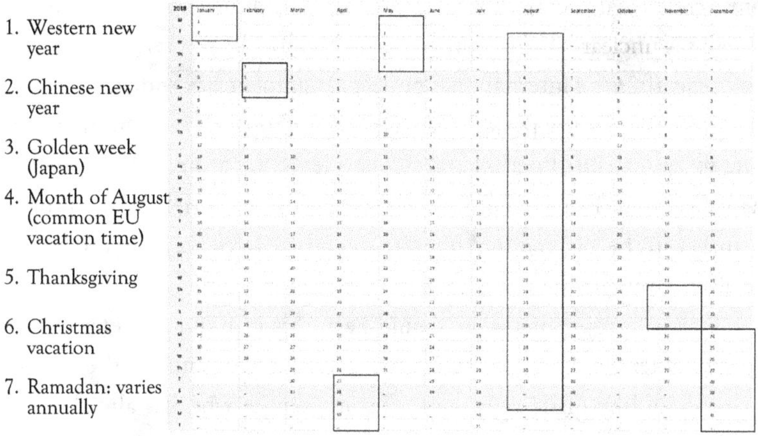

Figure 8.4 Global holiday calendar

While the Western project team may be shutting operations around December or January timeframe and become ready to start up and get back to business in late January early or February, this may be precisely the time the New Year's Day celebration is occurring in Asia. The final holiday schedule that may be unfamiliar to many Western project managers is that of Ramadan. Ramadan is observed in Islamic countries or in countries where Islam is the dominant culture and Ramadan is a holiday that shifts from year to year since it is based on the lunar calendar. There is no one specific date when Ramadan is being observed at the same time every year, so it is something to consider when preparing for important project milestones in an Islamic country.

Culture Shock

Project managers and team members can find it very unsettling to have to live and work in a foreign country for an extended period of time. This phenomenon is known as culture shock. Culture shock can hit immediately after arriving in a foreign country. The intense feelings of culture shock may improve after time passes, but may become stronger, especially during the wintertime perhaps when depression can set in. Project managers and team members must be aware of the phenomenon of culture shock when making long-term assignments for a global project. It does not help in the culture change situation when an expatriate assignment is open-ended. Further, culture shock becomes a more significant concern when it is unclear what the project team member or project manager will be doing after the international project assignment has ended. In such a case, it is easy for the project manager to lose hope to be in the alien culture for an extended period and perhaps leave the project. The situation happens often. Perhaps not only because of the shock felt by the project manager in the alien culture but also due to the stress experienced by the family accompanying the project manager (Figure 8.5).

A global project manager should keep this in mind and ensure that in any extended assignment involving a foreign country, the assignment should be made only with a team member who has already been to that country and perhaps has already experienced an extended stay. Moving to a foreign country for an extended stay prior to having experienced any of that country's culture is a very difficult move. Also, if the only available team member is the one who has not visited or lived in the foreign country prior to an extended assignment, it is highly recommended to send the team member there a few times for perhaps a couple of weeks at a time in order to become more familiarized with the local culture. Finally, it is good practice in an overseas assignment to allow return visits to the home country. When this policy is employed, the travelling team member will be advised regarding the number of visits home, how many are allowed by policy, how often, and then finally, the timeframe to return home as well as the role of the team member upon returning to the home country.

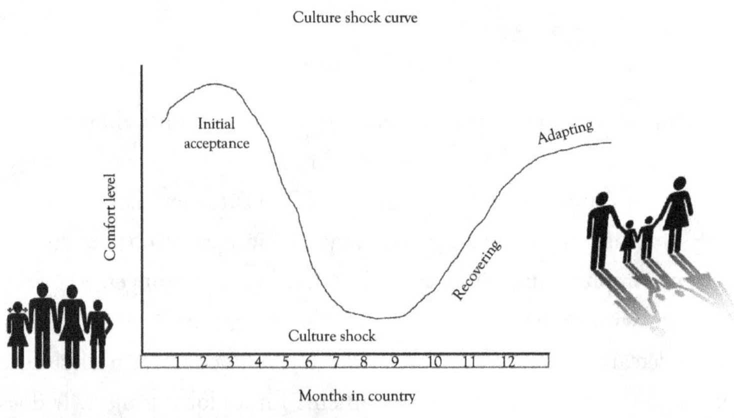

Figure 8.5 The culture shock curve

Culture Shock and Family

A project manager or team member may become familiar with a geographically distant country and culture, but it may be quite a different matter for the family. When sending a team member to another country with a different culture, it is important to consider whether the family will fare well in a different culture. It is also preferred to send only families who have some familiarity with the culture of the assigned country. The project sponsor should consider if the family of the team member being sent to another country has traveled abroad before and had experiences with other cultures. Another consideration might be the age of the children. Also, the project manager should determine if the spouse is employed and to what extent will moving to a different country affect her employment and overall financial situation. The question of whether a project team member can thrive in a distant country and another culture therefore goes far beyond an assessment of the individual but also includes family members. Finally, if the family is apparently ready and willing to move to a different country, there is also the consideration of additional expense. Can the project team afford to send an entire family overseas for an extended period and absorb this expense? Or is it better to ask a team member to visit the foreign country for several short stays over a period of several months perhaps 1–2 weeks at a time? (Figure 8.6).

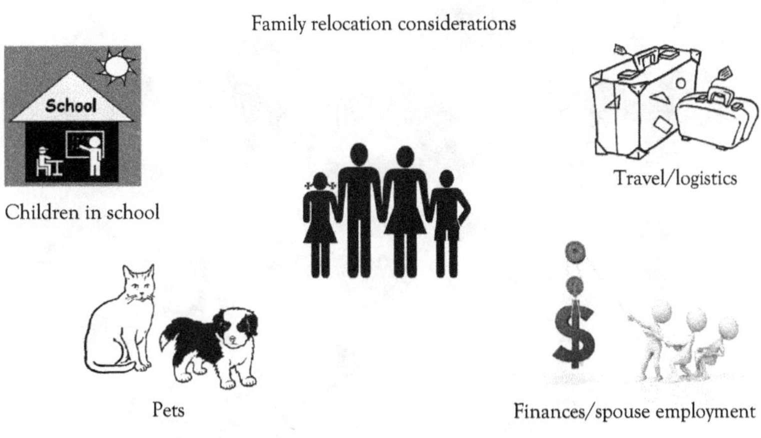

Figure 8.6 Family relocation considerations

The important thing to remember is that it is never as simple as it may seem to send the team member to another country. There are elements of culture, culture shock, logistics including family member employment, the schools that the children attend, and language and cultural transition difficulties. The list of difficulties and risk is nearly endless. As in all complex activity undertaken by the project team, global team member assignments must be planned as a subproject using the five process groups.

CHAPTER 9

Information Exchange

Project managers frequently communicate informally and perhaps very rapidly with team members in their own language in the home country. The day-to-day informal conversation back and forth between team members can lead to extensive use of informal and idiomatic expressions. This poses no problem between members of the same culture; however, when crossing cultures and communicating to non-native English speakers, the rapid use of informal conversational and idiomatic expressions could be a subject of much confusion. As an example, consider typical English expressions such as "hurry up," "calm down," "down in the dumps," "hands down," "keep your chin up," or "catch up." A native English speaker will immediately understand the intended meaning behind these idiomatic expressions. However, someone from another country who did not grow up speaking English may find such phrases confusing. For example, when the phrase "hurry up!" is expressed, it is not surprising to observe a non-native English speaker looking up. Or, when saying "calm down!" the term "calm" could be understood, but the term "down" may be unclear in this instance. Native English speakers understand that "down" does not really mean "down" in this case but is instead an idiomatic expression. As is the case with most idiomatic expressions however, it is one that does not clearly express the intended meaning to a non-native English speaker (Figure 9.1).

What this suggests is that project managers working with team members in other countries should simplify their communication and as much as possible avoid specialized and idiomatic expressions. Instead, use the simplest possible way of expressing a thought at all times. A fellow English speaker, upon hearing a project manager speaking to a non-native English speaker in a very simple way, may think of what is being expressed as "baby talk." If talking in a plain, simple, and direct manner helps communicate information clearly and succinctly, then it

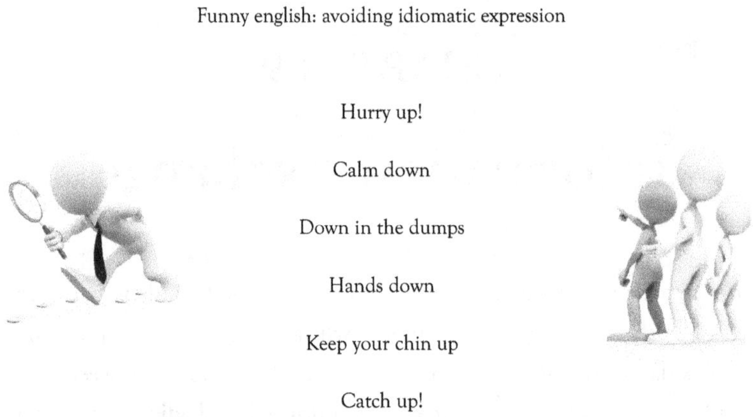

Funny english: avoiding idiomatic expression
Hurry up!
Calm down
Down in the dumps
Hands down
Keep your chin up
Catch up!

Figure 9.1 Avoid idiomatic expressions

is recommended to use it. Keeping in mind the mathematical expression of the "least common denominator," project managers should seek to be understood by that one person least able to understand English. This will naturally require a simplicity of expression without idiomatic expressions.

Deciphering Non-Native English Usage

The problem of communicating in a foreign country goes both ways. Native English speakers can confuse others by using idiomatic expressions, but on the other hand non-native English speakers can use what native speakers would consider to be "broken English." Do not be surprised when unusual usage patterns arise from non-native English speakers in conversations. These include phrases that do not necessarily make sense as well as occasional profanity. A non-native speaker of English may use profanity without being aware of its meaning or the shock it may cause when the word is spoken. Project managers are encouraged to be understanding when interacting with non-native English speakers and consider that their facility with English language may be limited. Because of this, sometimes some rather surprising expressions may appear in the conversation. The same is true of writing e-mails or documents. Upon receiving an e-mail that doesn't make sense or comes across as offensive, project managers are encouraged to take a deep breath and think about the possible intent behind the e-mail or message. It is advisable to pick up the phone or initiate a video conference and discuss the issue or hold a meeting with the individual who sent the e-mail prior to letting the situation become inflamed or result in unnecessary conflict (Figure 9.2).

Finally remember that when broken English is heard or perhaps a T-shirt with some unusual English expression is observed, avoid the temptation to laugh or mock. Remember also that it is not uncommon for native English speakers to wear shirts or pieces of jewelry with Chinese characters while being unaware of their meaning. Such a character may mean something that is offensive to those who can understand it but not offensive at all to an English speaker who has no idea what the symbol could mean. Also, when it comes to exchanging information, do not neglect the high-context versus low-context consideration. Some information may be more appropriate to be handled in a face-to-face meeting rather than an e-mail or conference call. Some communication should not take place at all unless the relationship is first developed. For example, sending an electronic survey to several team members residing within a high-context country will typically not yield very many responses. Responding to a survey devoid of the relationship context creates uncertainty and sometimes confusion. It is essential for the communication plan of a global project therefore to map the choices of media to the category of messages and direction that it is sent back and forth. The plan should also take into account elements of cultural dimensions as well as the differentiation between high- and low-context communication.

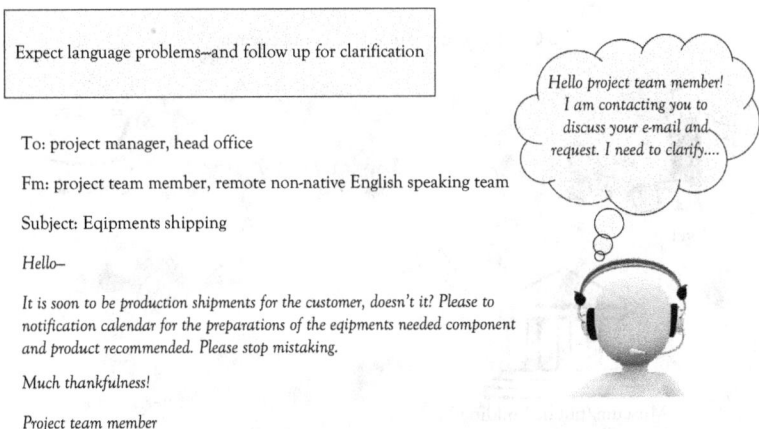

Expect language problems—and follow up for clarification

To: project manager, head office

Fm: project team member, remote non-native English speaking team

Subject: Eqipments shipping

Hello–

It is soon to be production shipments for the customer, doesn't it? Please to notification calendar for the preparations of the eqipments needed component and product recommended. Please stop mistaking.

Much thankfulness!

Project team member

Hello project team member!
I am contacting you to
discuss your e-mail and
request. I need to clarify....

Figure 9.2 Anticipating language problems

Connectivity

Communication in remote areas can only happen if there is appropriate media for sending and receiving information. The Internet is nearly ubiquitous, but it is important to keep in mind that some areas of the world lack Internet or lack the high-bandwidth Internet that is very common in developed countries. Project teams must consider this in advance and plan for how e-mail and transfer of files will take place in remote areas. For example, low-bandwidth Internet is enough for e-mails and there may be local telecommunications systems to satisfy the need for voice communication. However, there may be insufficient bandwidth to support teleconferencing or transferring of very large files (Figure 9.3).

It may be the case that the project team visits the client site to conduct an installation and discovers that the team needs a major software upgrade that can only be delivered through the Internet. What if this is a need that is foreseen but the connectivity at the local factory or job site is insufficient? It may be that in such a case the project team would need to return to the hotel if it is quite advanced in communication and has enough bandwidth capability, or perhaps go to a local restaurant, coffee shop, or Internet café. The key message for connectivity is to think ahead. Consider what action would need to be taken if the required bandwidth is not there and where are possible islands of bandwidth that the project team could take advantage of to get the job done when the need for bandwidth exists and the available options are few.

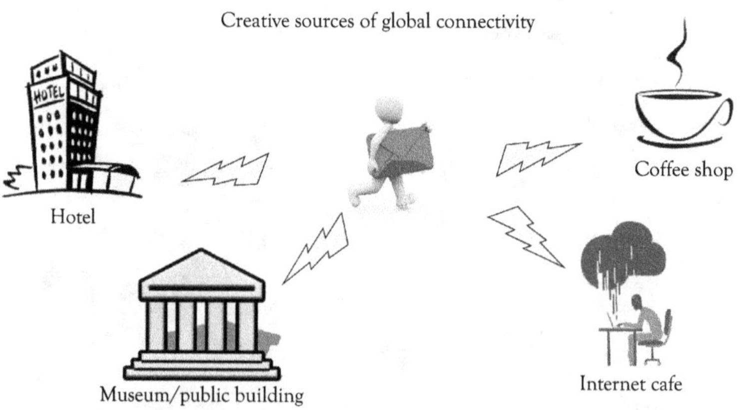

Figure 9.3 Sources of global connectivity

Nonverbal Communication

Differences in language and the complexity of expression that are often involved in the use of idiomatic expressions lead to a significant breakdown of communication. However, the spoken word is not the only communication channel used between project team members and stakeholders within other countries' regions and cultures. Nonverbal communication is always involved in face-to-face and in video conference call settings. Nonverbal communication involves facial expressions, posture, gestures, and even the tone in which something is spoken. Global project team members must be attuned to nonverbal cues that they send intentionally or unintentionally as well as those received by parties from different cultures. For example, it is not uncommon to sit in a meeting with Japanese stakeholders and see one or two meeting members apparently dozing off in the meeting. However, if the name of that individual is addressed, that person will suddenly perk up and respond immediately. When this behavior is observed, it is not necessarily an example of sleep but rather an example of contemplation. Likewise, it is not uncommon to have long periods of silence in a conversation within a high-context culture (Figure 9.4).

Western project managers are often confronted with long periods of silence and may seek to fill it by talking. This is rarely a good idea as the project manager may say too much or send the wrong message to the other

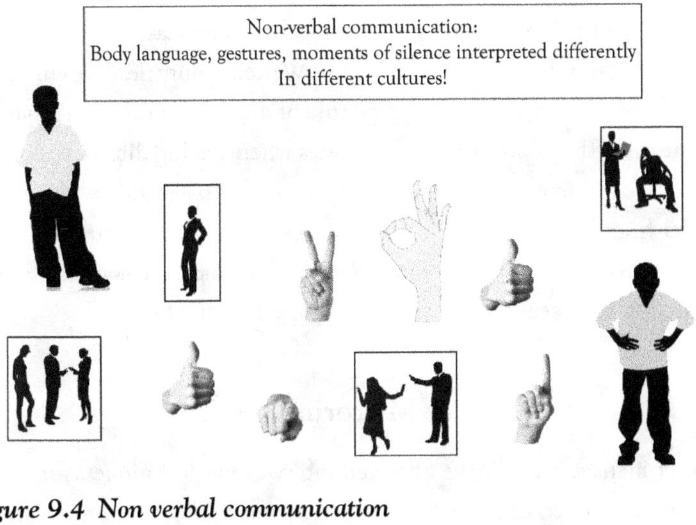

Non-verbal communication:
Body language, gestures, moments of silence interpreted differently
In different cultures!

Figure 9.4 Non verbal communication

part. The silence should be appreciated and often it is useful to mirror the behavior of the stakeholder who is the party to the communication. Gestures are another potential minefield for face-to-face communication between different cultures. Hand gestures that may have an innocuous meaning in the Western world may be interpreted as demeaning, insulting, or even profane in some cultures. Such gestures are not limited to the hands but also perhaps the shrug of the shoulders or a display of the soles of the feet. Project managers embarking on projects in other countries and cultures should do research to understand which gestures are acceptable and which should be avoided. If possible, discuss the matter with a national or local from the country with which the project team is expected to do business and ask detailed questions. On the other side of this equation, it is important to avoid misinterpreting gestures, posture, or other nonverbal cues from the stakeholder from a different culture and take offense. For example, it is not uncommon in Asian countries to be in a conversation with another party and to observe the person holding his or her arms folded tightly across the chest. From a Western perspective, this might be interpreted as the person being resistant or adamant with respect to a point. Although this may be the inference taken, it may not mean that all in the other culture. It may simply be a relaxed position and therefore an indication of an expression of interest. In addition to being careful about posture, periods of silence, tone of voice, and gestures, don't read too much into other nonverbal cues that may be misinterpreted as something negative when they are, in fact, not. A final aspect of nonverbal communication is eye contact. In many Western countries, eye contact is considered very important. It is a gesture of directness and often a symbol of integrity. This is not true in all cultures where having direct eye contact could be considered impolite. If an engaging in conversation with a stakeholder from another culture and limited eye contact is detected, this may be a cultural artifact rather than example of the individual attempting to mislead or to deceive as it may be interpreted in the West.

Mirroring

Project managers who have observed interviewing techniques, for example, in the context of a television crime drama, will often notice that the interrogator when asking questions of the witness may tend to mirror the behaviors of the witness. In this context, if the interviewee leans back in the chair so does the interviewer. If the interviewee puts his chin on his or her hand and leans forward so does the interviewer. Also, if the subject being interviewed pauses and does not speak for a while, the interviewer typically also does not talk and lets the silence pass. The approach of mirroring is a reasonable one for project managers in global teams communicating across cultures. This is especially true when interacting with stakeholders who are not native English speakers. It is best to be patient, remain quiet and reserved, and in the absence of being able to speak the language seek to behave in a manner that best represents the local culture. In fact, behaving similarly to others within that local culture may be preferred over attempting to speak the language (Figure 9.5).

For example, having a Westerner attempt to speak Chinese in the People's Republic of China will likely catch a Chinese national off guard and may seem strange to the Chinese national at first. Further, it is highly likely that attempting such a maneuver will lead to mistakes, some of which may be embarrassing. This leaves project team members with the overall communication advice of mirroring local behaviors, remaining quiet calm and reserved, and avoid straying into unfamiliar areas. Take special care when attempting to speak an unfamiliar language. Language and culture is a very deep well. If the project team

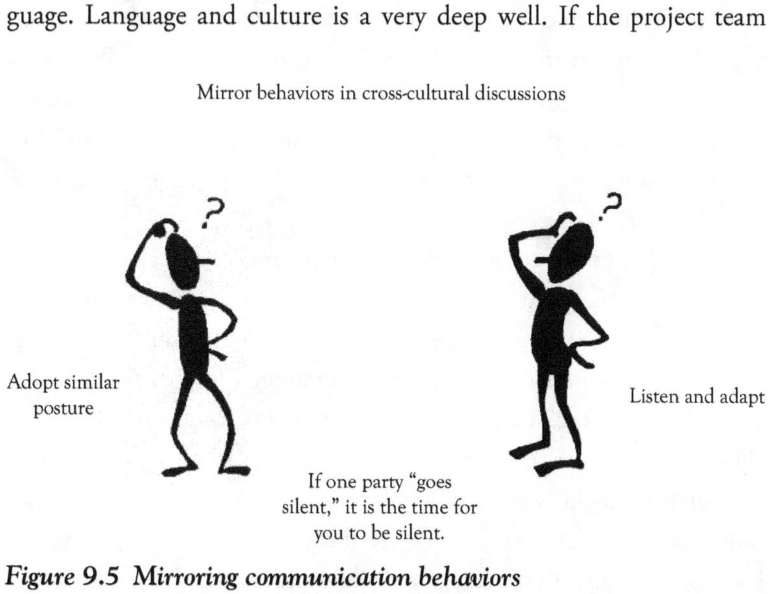
Mirror behaviors in cross-cultural discussions
?
?
Adopt similar posture
Listen and adapt
If one party "goes silent," it is the time for you to be silent.

Figure 9.5 Mirroring communication behaviors

member has not grown up with the culture and is not fluent in the language from an early age, then the team member is only exposed to a drop in the bucket compared to an ocean of underlying know-how and meaning. It is unlikely that a project team member project manager will be able to fully tap into this cultural body of knowledge. It is therefore preferred to remain reserved, speak through an interpreter, or by using the native language of the project team including very simple basic terminology.

Negotiation

The natural give-and-take of negotiation is an important facet of any project. Negotiation is also part of life in global projects. The unique difficulties associated with negotiation in international projects is that different cultures have different approaches to the natural back-and-forth bargaining and discussion that occurs within a negotiation. High-context cultures require a period of getting to know one another prior to even beginning the commercial discussion that takes place in the negotiation context. Further, it is essential to expect that the other party to the negotiation may sit in silence for a few minutes after a proposal. As is the case in day-to-day conversations, Western team members inevitably attempt to fill periods of silence with talk and such unneeded talk may cause negotiations to become unraveled. Also, a period of silence may lead to multiple concessions that are unnecessary. What is necessary is to understand that different cultures may tend to respond to comments in a negotiation, an offer, or a counteroffer in ways that are unexpected (Figure 9.6).

A significant difficulty faced by Western project managers in global projects is the fact that some cultures are not able to disagree or to say "no" in a direct fashion. Project managers from low-context countries who are more familiar with a more direct approach in communication may believe that the other party to the negotiation has agreed with something when, in fact, no agreement exists at all. Often the difficulty of obtaining a straight "yes or no" answer is related to the fact that no single individual may make the decision for the group within the context of a collectivist culture. In the case of a major decision, an individual within a

Global client/vendor
• Initial informal discussion
• General introduction to negotiation topics
• Silent pauses for consideration
• Requests
• Objections
Project team
• Go with the flow of discussion
• Avoid getting too specific too early
• Match silence with silence
• Avoid jumping too quickly to offer and counter offer
• Discuss objections without over-reaction

Figure 9.6 Getting started in international negotiations

collectivist culture may need to propose the idea, socialize it, hold several meetings about it, and continue to interact within the organization until a consensus position finally emerges. Upon the project manager hearing a quick "yes or no" within a project negotiation, it bears remembering that an individual response may in reality mean little until the entire group, which the individual represents, has had an opportunity to weigh in and achieve consensus. Above all, the additional variables encountered in negotiations in the global environment reinforce the dictum that "patience is a virtue." An agreement that works for both sides is likely to take time to gel.

Common Goals in Global Negotiations

While significant differences exist on each side of the table between negotiating parties in global negotiations, it is important to understand what both sides are likely to have in common. Each party may be constrained by its cultural norms with respect to what is said as well how it is expressed. However, it is essential to remember that for both sides, negotiation is an exercise in trading. Trading between cultures is an activity that has existed from the dawn of time. With the perspective of trading in mind, global project teams can view project negotiations as a form of problem solving. Each side is at the negotiation table to fill a business need. Further, each side has access to resources that are valued less than the resources that each side seeks to fill. Negotiation is therefore an exercise in trading what is less needed for that which is most needed. When both sides of the table can achieve this, the negotiation is a success.

With the goals of the negotiation firmly in mind, the project team can prepare for the negotiation meeting by documenting answers to the following questions:

1. What are the goals of the negotiation?
2. What specific needs do we expect to fill in this negotiation?
3. What resources do we have that we would be willing to trade?
4. What are some specific trades we may attempt to offer?

Further, to prepare for the negotiation meeting, the project team should consider the same questions but from the perspective of the other negotiating party. For example:

1. What goals does the other party of the negotiation seek to achieve?
2. What specific needs does the other party of the negotiation seek to fill in this negotiation?
3. What resources does the other party have that they would be likely be willing to trade?
4. What are some specific trade-offs do we think that the other negotiation party may attempt to offer? (Figure 9.7).

The answers to each of the questions asked from both sides result in what could be viewed as a "negotiation plan." Beginning a negotiation meeting with a negotiation plan in place can aid global project managers by helping

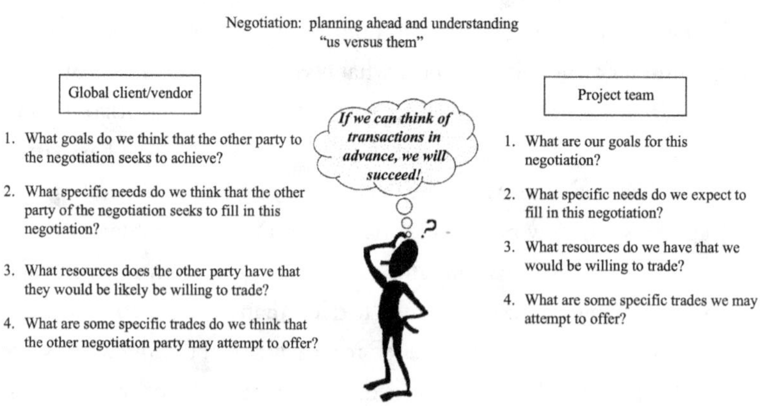
Negotiation: planning ahead and understanding "us versus them"
Global client/vendor
1. What goals do we think that the other party to the negotiation seeks to achieve?
2. What specific needs do we think that the other party of the negotiation seeks to fill in this negotiation?
3. What resources does the other party have that they would be likely be willing to trade?
4. What are some specific trades do we think that the other negotiation party may attempt to offer?
If we can think of transactions in advance, we will succeed!
Project team
1. What are our goals for this negotiation?
2. What specific needs do we expect to fill in this negotiation?
3. What resources do we have that we would be willing to trade?
4. What are some specific trades we may attempt to offer?

Figure 9.7 Planning ahead in negotiation

them stay focused on the goals without getting distracted by significant differences in approach exhibited within cross-cultural negotiations.

Managing a Cross-Cultural Project Negotiation

The first step in managing a cross-cultural negotiation is to determine the location for the negotiation. Recall that in international travel it is often easier to travel west when attending an important international meeting scheduled the next morning following arrival at the distant geographical location. Therefore, when planning a negotiation with a global project stakeholder or supplier, if the team has the option to choose a location outside of the country, it is recommended that the team select a location that allows for the negotiating party to travel west. Traveling west helps the visiting team feel more refreshed and relaxed during the first morning. Conversely, the other negotiation partner who had to travel east faces the difficulty of waking up far earlier than her normal schedule would allow for.

The next item involved in managing the negotiation is selecting the actual venue or room in which negotiations take place. Note that some cultures prefer table that is positioned in such a way that the person sitting faces the door as it opens. For example, it is common for dinner meetings in China to have a table so that host can sit and face the door. This may be something that those preparing for the meetings need to keep in mind. Consider also the seating arrangements at the table (Figure 9.8).

While it is common in Western countries to have the head of the company sit at the end of a long board room table, it is more typical in Asian countries to have the leadership take the center of the table. Likewise, the next highest in rank sits at the left and right hand of the leader who is seated at the center of the table. This is an essential aspect of arranging the table and failure to arrange it appropriately will cause confusion and embarrassment, and it may be taken as an offence by the negotiating partner. As a courtesy, once table setting arrangements have been made, it may be beneficial to provide a seating arrangement layout map to negotiating counterparts for review and approval before finalizing seating arrangements.

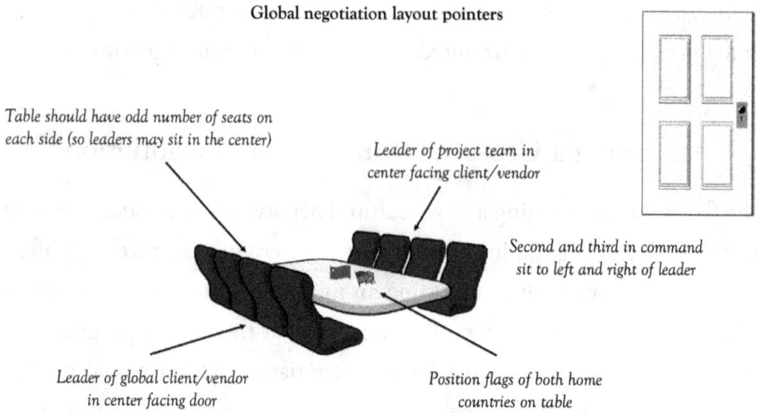
Global negotiation layout pointers
Table should have odd number of seats on each side (so leaders may sit in the center)
Leader of project team in center facing client/vendor
Second and third in command sit to left and right of leader
Leader of global client/vendor in center facing door
Position flags of both home countries on table

Figure 9.8 Global negotiation layout

Managing the Setting of the Negotiation

When the day arrives for the negotiation and both negotiating parties begin arriving, consider the fact that members of the other side of the table may be from a high-context culture or may be a mix of high- and low-context cultures. If this is the case, it is better to avoid negotiation prior to having some pre-meetings. An example of pre-meetings could include a dinner on the evening before the negotiations and possibly several meetings in advance in order to build that friendship. Given some context to the negotiating meeting has been established, when both parties arrive at the meeting room, it is common to present business cards to each other. Pay attention to the exchange of business cards, particularly in Asian countries. Changing business cards can be highly ceremonial and the card is often considered the extension of the individual who owns it. Therefore when a business card is received, accept the card with both hands and examine it carefully. Do not immediately place it in the pocket, but hold it and play close attention to it. It is considered polite to ask questions about the card, pronounce the name, and acknowledge the title. Likewise, when presenting a business card, present it with both hands as a gesture of respect to the other side. After initial greetings in the exchange of cards, when it is time for the project manager take the seat at the table, arrange the cards on the table, put them in order of rank, and make note of the cards and individuals. Acknowledge that

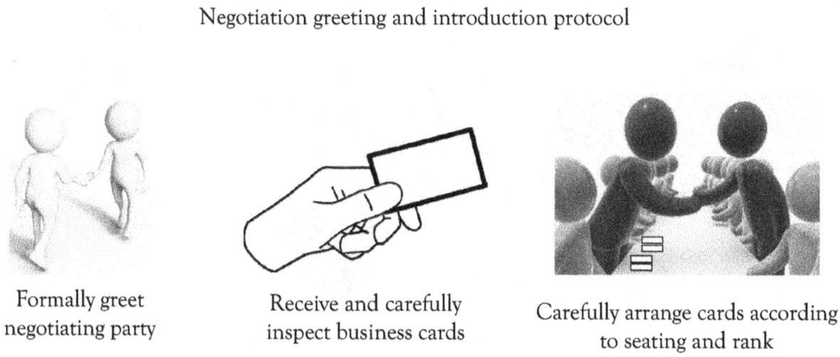
Negotiation greeting and introduction protocol
Formally greet negotiating party
Receive and carefully inspect business cards
Carefully arrange cards according to seating and rank

Figure 9.9 Greeting and introductions in negotiation

it is recognized which card belongs to whom to as well as where is the corresponding person seated around the table. This is a gesture of respect (Figure 9.9).

Once both negotiating parties are seated, it is time for the negotiation discussions to begin. Since there may be a mix of people from high- and low-context cultures present, it is best not to start directly into a discussion of business. Instead talk about the weather, family members, sports, or other trivial matters to take a little time to warm up the meeting room. Perhaps introduce some light humor and get the conversation going. After adding this dash of informality to the process, gradually bring the topic around to the subject at hand. In the beginning stages of negotiation, it is best to talk in very general terms about what the goals are perhaps and understand what possible goals of the other side may be. Speak in general terms what it is that the team seeks to accomplish in this negotiation and what the project team may be willing to trade in return for it. Keep in mind though that the initial discussions are intended to be exploratory in nature. Eventually the conversation becomes more in-depth and serious. Details may begin to flow from the initial general exchange of information. Take care not to rush this process. It may be a good idea to bring in a white board, preferably one that prints out what has been captured on the board. Use this to capture key points for print out and review. These activities then eventually lead to proposals and then eventually to offers. The main principle is to be patient, to avoid talking during periods of silence, and to avoid revising proposals or offers during extended periods of silence.

CHAPTER 10

Financial Matters

An experienced CFO (Chief Financial Officer) can be a big help in deciding how the project is to be funded when the work is carried out in many distributed geographical locations. Some basic questions to be asked include, "What is the source of funding in what currency will we pay for materials and labor and components?" Also, "What are the regulations associated with bringing in money and moving money out of (and between) different geographical locations?" Finally, the CFO will need to advise the project team about concerns such as currency fluctuations in countries in which the project team is working. For example, assume the global project manager managing a team that won a bid in a foreign country and the bid is for an information system that requires installation. The bid was one based upon an initial budget that included analysis of costs, but such a budget may not have included all eventualities of currency fluctuation. In the early stage of the project, therefore, it may be recommended to put a currency hedge in place to protect against fluctuations. Another important concern is obtaining payment from the client and ensuring that the client will pay for the products and services that the project provides. One way to do this is through the mechanism of "letter of credit" (LC) (Figure 10.1).

The letter of credit is a financial instrument created between a customer in the geographically distant country along with the local bank of the client. The bank confirms that the client has the funds to pay for the deliverables. Further, the contractual terms are put in place such that when the project team meets its obligations for deliverables, the funding associated with the contractual terms are then released. The letter of credit therefore is a way of securing payment when it otherwise might be unclear whether the client has the means or if the client is likely to follow through with contractual fiduciary obligations.

CFO support for global projects

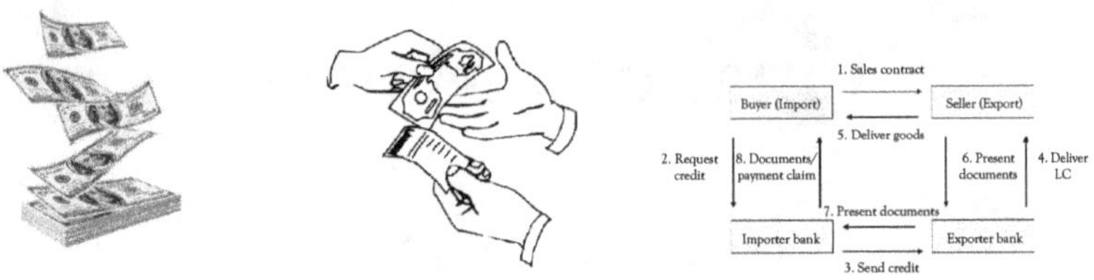

Manage currency fluctuations

Cash flow between regions

Managing letter of credit process

Figure 10.1 The letter of credit

Taxation

Another way the CFO can aid the project team is in providing advice on taxation. For example, a project that involves an installation in a foreign country and involves importing many pieces of equipment may be subject to significant import duties. This may require some creativity in order to be managed. Some Latin American countries, for example, have very high import duties on electronics products. However, such duties drop considerably when at least some work is done by local labor between the importing of the product and its destination to the local customer. It may be less expensive to import products and subsystems and have a local team test them, label them, and package them for the local market rather than import 100 percent finished goods (Figure 10.2).

The cost of labor may be less than the cost of import duties. Another approach to addressing this challenge of import duties is to import within a more favorable country first. Consider as an example a project team based in China importing to the European Union (EU). Such a project team would experience high import duties importing finished goods into the EU. However, if subsystems are imported to a country with low local labor cost (e.g., the Czech Republic) and completed systems are manufactured at this interim operation, these in turn can be exported to the rest of the EU at much lower import duties than if the product came from China directly. As is the case of the Latin American example, this is a matter of comparing the costs of local labor versus the cost incurred by the import

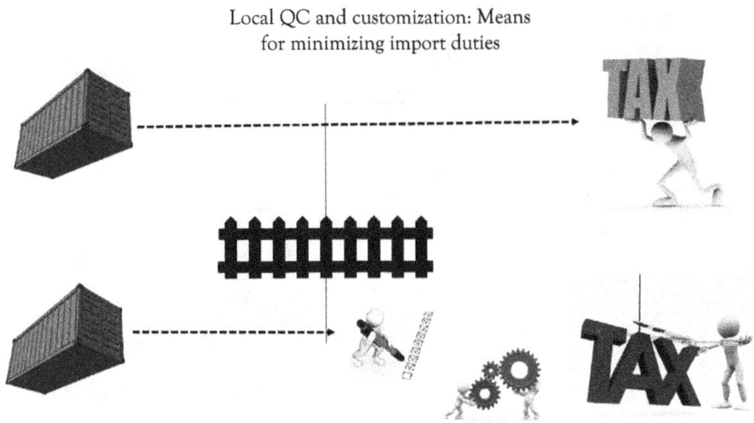

Figure 10.2 Minimizing import duties

duties. In many cases the cost of local labor expended at some level of customization to produce finish systems of subsystems may be much less than import duties.

The Big Mac Index

How much does it really cost to live or to do business in a foreign country? One of the ways to answer this is to compare the value of currency of the home country to the country in which the project team seeks to do project business. The principle that applies in evaluating currency values in global projects is the concept of *purchase price parity* (PPP). Using PPP, it is possible to deduce to what extent currency is overvalued or undervalued by comparing the price of common goods in both countries and then comparing this against the exchange rate. Often this is done formally by comparing the price of the basket of commodities between two countries. However, the *The Economist* magazine has created a simple method to do this, which is both humorous as well as effective. To explain the approach of the *The Economist,* consider for example what might be found in a theoretical "basket of commodities" compared between countries. The comparison may include the cost of local labor, the cost to rent or buy property in which to do business, and local agricultural products such as grains, vegetables, dairy, and poultry, to name just a few. A simple way to compare such a bundle of commodities is to compare the price

Using the "Big Mac Index" as a determinant of purchasing power

Hmm...I overpay for countries <1...

Big Mac index - global prices for a Big Mac 2018	Average (USD)	Index
Switzerland	6.8	1.28
Norway	6.2	1.17
Sweden	6.1	1.15
Finland	5.6	1.06
Canada	5.3	1.00
United States	5.3	1.00
Italy	5.1	0.96
France	5.1	0.96
Brazil	5.1	0.96
Ireland	5	0.94
Belgium	5	0.94
Denmark	4.9	0.92
Uruguay	4.9	0.92
Israel	4.8	0.91
Germany	4.8	0.91
Spain	4.8	0.91
Euro area	4.8	0.91
Australia	4.7	0.89
Netherlands	4.5	0.85
New Zealand	4.5	0.85
Singapore	4.4	0.83
Britain	4.4	0.83
Chile	4.3	0.81
Austria	4.2	0.79
Greece	4.1	0.77
South Korea	4.1	0.77
Costa Rica	4	0.75
Argentina	4	0.75
Estonia	3.9	0.74
Portugal	3.9	0.74
Sri Lanka	3.8	0.72
Colombia	3.8	0.72
UAE	3.8	0.72

Divide local dollar price by US price for index

Big Mac Index, 2018

Figure 10.3 The Big Mac Index

of the big Mac Hamburger from one country to another (Figure 10.3) (*The Economist* 2019).

The Economist magazine does this and publishes a scale known as the big Mac index. The big Mac index compares price of Big Macs across many different countries and compares that to the currency exchange rate with the base currency, in this case the US dollar. When examining the prices of Big Macs around the world, it is easy to see which countries likely have overvalued versus undervalued currency.

Responding to the Big Mac Index

As interesting is and as humorous as the big Mac index is, it begs the question, "What should global project managers do with this kind of information?" The degree to which a local currency is overvalued or undervalued goes a long way toward informing the project team where work should be done, labor should be hired, and facilities be established. As an example, if the home country currency is overvalued, the local country may be a preferred location for the team to develop deliverables for the project. The local country may also be the preferred location for hiring labor to carry out a major installation. Overvaluation in the home country shows that the home country currency could go much further in the geographically remote country than in the home country. If this is the case, it makes

The Big Mac Index as indication of local spending benefit
Better to use local labor if operating in countries <1...

Big Mac index - global prices for a Big Mac 2018	Average (USD)	Index
Switzerland	6.8	1.28
Norway	6.2	1.17
Sweden	6.1	1.15
Finland	5.6	1.06
Canada	5.3	1.00
United States	5.3	1.00
Italy	5.1	0.96
France	5.1	0.96
Brazil	5.1	0.96
Ireland	5	0.94
Belgium	5	0.94
Denmark	4.9	0.92
Uruguay	4.9	0.92
Israel	4.8	0.91
Germany	4.8	0.91
Spain	4.8	0.91
Euro area	4.8	0.91
Australia	4.7	0.89
Netherlands	4.5	0.85
New Zealand	4.5	0.85
Singapore	4.4	0.83
Britain	4.4	0.83
Chile	4.3	0.81
Austria	4.2	0.79
Greece	4.1	0.77
South Korea	4.1	0.77
Costa Rica	4	0.75
Argentina	4	0.75
Estonia	3.9	0.74
Portugal	3.9	0.74
Sri Lanka	3.8	0.72
Colombia	3.8	0.72
UAE	3.8	0.72

Big Mac Index, 2018

Figure 10.4 Applying the Big Mac Index

much more sense to hire local labor, lease local facilities, and do as much business as possible in the local currency (Figure 10.4).

If the reverse is true, for example, the geographically distant location has an overvalued currency compared to the home country, it may make more sense to minimize local hiring and send the project team members from the home country to live in the local country to compensate for the differences in currency valuation. A final consideration is to think about how the big Mac index has changed over time. If the project is expected to last for more than 12–18 months, it may be wise to understand the pattern of currency fluctuation over the past several years within that local country. Once the project team has established a strategy to manage valuation differences of currency between home country in the local country, it is best to avoid a major shift in strategy because of the sudden change in currency valuation. This has been known to happen in some countries. One example of this occurred several years ago in Venezuela. In 2010, there was a sudden 100 percent devaluation of the currency in Venezuela. Any project producing deliverables during this time would experience significant shock to the business plan if the project team is not prepared. This is an example of the financial risk that a project manager will need to keep in mind and think about carefully when assigning teams around the globe and making the decision between the degree to which the team uses labor, materials, and capital from the home country versus the geographically distant country.

Commercial Terms

International commercial terms are provided in contracts in order to indicate specifically where transfer of title or ownership of a piece of property occurs. Assume, for example, a project team is managing a project in Europe and is shipping a major hardware component from a port in the United States such as New Jersey. Both parties in this transaction must know where transfer of title of the deliverables occur. If the terms include "FOB New Jersey" in the contract, this is a reference to "free on board," which indicates that the transfer of title occurs when the equipment is placed on board the transport at the port from which it is shipping, in this case New Jersey. Prior to the equipment loaded onto the ship, the project team that produced the deliverables holds the title to the deliverables. Once the equipment is loaded on the ship however, the title is transferred to the client (if FOB commercial terms are so indicated). This means that in the case of a disaster where the ship sinks and the equipment is lost, it is not a loss to the project team. Once the title has transferred upon shipping, then payment according to contractual terms are now due from the client to the project team. It is incumbent upon the client to have insurance on the deliverables so that they are secure throughout the transport from, in this case, the port of New Jersey to the final destination in Europe. Global project managers must pay close attention to terms such as free on board. Another common international commercial term is "Ex-Factory" or "Ex-Works." This indicates that title transfer of the deliverable occurs once it leaves the factory. If a project team is ordering component or subsystems as part of the integration a larger system, if, for example, the contract stipulates "Ex-Factory" or "Ex-Works," then the project team must be aware that it is responsible for transporting the goods and that title to the goods is transferred to the project team once it left the factory. As a final note, FOB terms are quite common as EX works in X factory as the location of transfer of title is often so indicated on the contract (Figure 10.5) (Nscontainer.com 2019).

For example, FOB Tokyo, FOB Munich, or Ex-Factory with reference to specific factory or ex-works with reference to a specific operation indicates the location at which the title is transferred. From there, the receiving party (the client, or the project team ordering components,

International Commercial Terms Reference Chart

TERM	EXW	FCA	FAS	FOB	CFR	CIF	CPT	CIP	DAF	DES	DEQ	DDU	DDP
	Ex-works	Free carrier	Free alongside ship	Free on-board vessel	Cost and freight	Cost insurance & freight	Carriage paid to	Carriage & insurance paid to	Delivery at frontier	Delivered ex-ship	Delivered ex-quay, duty unpaid	delivered Duty unpaid	delivered duty paid
SERVICE	Who Pays	Who Pays	Who Pays	Who Pays	Who Pays	Who Pays	Who Pays	Who Pays	Who Pays	Who Pays	Who Pays	Who Pays	Who Pays
Warehouse storage at point of origin	Seller	Seller	Seller	Seller	Seller	Seller	Seller	Seller	Seller	Seller	Seller	Seller	Seller
Warehouse labor at point of origin	Seller	Seller	Seller	Seller	Seller	Seller	Seller	Seller	Seller	Seller	Seller	Seller	Seller
Export packing	Seller	Seller	Seller	Seller	Seller	Seller	Seller	Seller	Seller	Seller	Seller	Seller	Seller
Loading at point of origin	Buyer	Seller	Seller	Seller	Seller	Seller	Seller	Seller	Seller	Seller	Seller	Seller	Seller
Inland freight	Buyer	Buyer	Seller	Seller	Seller	Seller	Seller	Seller	Seller	Seller	Seller	Seller	Seller
Port receiving charges	Buyer	Buyer	Seller	Seller	Seller	Seller	Seller	Seller	Seller	Seller	Seller	Seller	Seller
Forwarders fee	Buyer	Buyer	Seller	Seller	Seller	Seller	Seller	Seller	Seller	Seller	Seller	Seller	Seller
Loading on ocean carrier	Buyer	Buyer	Buyer	Seller	Seller	Seller	Seller	Seller	Seller	Seller	Seller	Seller	Seller
Ocean/Air freight charges	Buyer	Buyer	Buyer	Buyer	Seller	Seller	Seller	Seller	Seller	Seller	Seller	Seller	Seller
Charges at foreign Port/Airport	Buyer	Buyer	Buyer	Buyer	Buyer	Buyer	Seller	Seller	Seller	Buyer	Seller	Seller	Seller
Customs, Duties and Taxes abroad	Buyer	Buyer	Buyer	Buyer	Buyer	Buyer	Buyer	Buyer	Buyer	Buyer	Buyer	Buyer	Seller
Delivery charges to final destination	Buyer	Buyer	Buyer	Buyer	Buyer	Buyer	Buyer	Buyer	Buyer	Buyer	Buyer	Seller	Seller

(North Star Container 2018)

Figure 10.5 International commercial terms

materials, or equipment) takes ownership of the deliverable and it must ensure the safety of the components' transport. Further, the receiving party must bear the cost from that FOB location to the ultimate destination. In contract negotiations, attention paid to contractual terms may make the difference between profit and loss. For example, if a subsystem ordered by a project team is manufactured in Tokyo, but the project team does not want the additional expense of insurance or trouble of transporting it from Tokyo, then a local FOB location could be secured as part of the contract. These are just a few examples of international commercial terms for which a global project team must be aware. Neglect of international commercial terms could be quite costly so it much be considered in the plan and in the execution of the global project plan.

Logistics and Delivery

In addition to the commercial terms in the contract for deliverables, global project teams are well advised to think through the logistics of shipping deliverables from one location to another. In major capital projects for example, it is important to evaluate if there is enough shipping and receiving infrastructure at the location where the project will be installed. Also, circumstances may call for the use of heavy equipment. However, heavy equipment may only be employed if the site can support it. The team must be able to answer further logistics-related questions such as, "Can the product being delivered be taken from ship loaded onto a train or truck and then delivered?" and "Could some portions of the deliverables be flown?" Also, "How difficult or expensive is it to move parts and equipment to the ultimate destination?"

There are locations that are difficult to reach by any means so as a recommendation the project team could consider employing a checklist to ensure that the team has thought through logistical difficulties for moving parts, equipment, and even people from one location to another. Another concern with logistics concerns the role of customs. How easy or difficult is it to get the parts or components and labor for shipping from one country to another? Does it require special intervention by local agents or legal professionals? How accurate does the paperwork need to be and what happens if there are errors in the customs paperwork? (Figure 10.6).

Logistics and customs
Consider how to legally move equipment, components, or deliverables in and out of remote areas

Figure 10.6 Logistics and customs

Logistics is an area of risk analysis where it pays to consider scenarios of what could possibly go wrong. Finally, there may be regulations on the type of equipment that can and cannot enter a country. Further, even if the equipment being used by the project meets such requirements, if it is close to the borderline of being a problem, it may remain in customs for an extended period for enhanced inspection. Also, there will be times when an important component or piece of software or piece of equipment or tools may need to be rapidly shipped to the global project destination to address an urgent concern. In such a case is it even possible to expedite such goods through local customs? What actions could the project team take if there are no means for expediting the entry of parts, components, tools, and equipment through local customs? Unfortunately, some project teams who have encountered such an urgent situation with little other recourse may attempt to bring parts, components, or tools into the country by themselves perhaps on a commercial flight. This is a dangerous practice as it could lead to fines, arrest, or even imprisonment. Always remember that project teams are the guests in other countries. Failure to follow the rules could end up with severe penalties. Throughout all PMBOK processes, there is an emphasis on "plan first, then do." This is most important when it comes to thinking through how to move goods and supplies from the home country to the end destination and to navigate through the rocky shoals of local customs officers.

CHAPTER 11

Ethics and Corruption

Behavior that is considered appropriate in one part of the world or culture may not be viewed that way in another. This is a question of ethics and ethical practices tend to vary across a spectrum of different viewpoints, traditions, and cultures. The question for global project teams is to consider which practices to follow. One way to do this is to consider various ethics-related scenarios in advance and think through possible responses along with the rationale behind those responses. One of the more common issues faced by global project managers is the question of bribery. Bribery is not only an ethical issue, but a legal one that is addressed by the Foreign Corrupt Practices Act within the United States. Setting aside legal concerns, if a project manager was solicited for a bribe in another country—and it was a condition of doing business—should the project manager pay the bribe, or not? The obvious response would appear to be a resounding "no!" However, what if failing to pay the bribe led to the closure of the project and as a result, over fifty people would lose their jobs? Would this be an example of a situation in which paying a bribe would be warranted? Simply asking this question assumes an *ontological* ethical perspective. An ontological or utilitarian approach is commonly used in business because, like most activities in business, it employs a "cost–benefit" analysis. If bribery is analyzed in this manner, the possible penalty associated with getting caught and punished for bribery is weighed against the benefit of a successful project and the maintaining of employment for a significant number of people. The *deontological* approach to ethical thinking considers the duty of one who is bound to "do the right thing." It is the act itself that is ethical or unethical regardless of potential costs or benefits to any party. Therefore, bribery, being fundamentally unethical, is not an appropriate subject for analysis using the cost–benefit approach. Criticisms exist for viewing ethics from a cost–benefit perspective outside of the deontological perspective.

Such criticism states that those evaluating an ethical matter by comparing costs and benefits will never be able to fully capture the totality of costs versus benefits. Because of this, cost–benefit based decisions are always imperfect and possibly erroneous in most circumstances (Figure 11.1) (Velasquez, and Velasquez 2002).

Bribery, project success, and the "job-saving" example illustrates the gray areas that exist in the spectrum of behaviors encountered in the global environment. Further, "bribery versus jobs" may seem rather innocuous. However, consider a different example of a global project team deciding whether to incorporate an additional safety precaution on a component used in a project deliverable. The ontological approach would involve consideration of the potential legal costs faced by the sponsor of the project should the component contribute to an accident or disaster. Such costs would be compared to cost of designing the component with additional safety precautions in the first place. The project team using cost–benefit approach would select the lowest cost option. Since human life is involved, this approach does seem inherently inappropriate for an ontological approach.

Is bribery therefore acceptable in the global environment, or not? It is clearly illegal, but it can also be a way of life in less developed countries and most project teams will encounter the issue. When the issue does arise and is discussed, consider that disagreements regarding action may result from differences in thinking that ultimately arise from the ontological–deontological dichotomy. In the spirit of project planning, a global

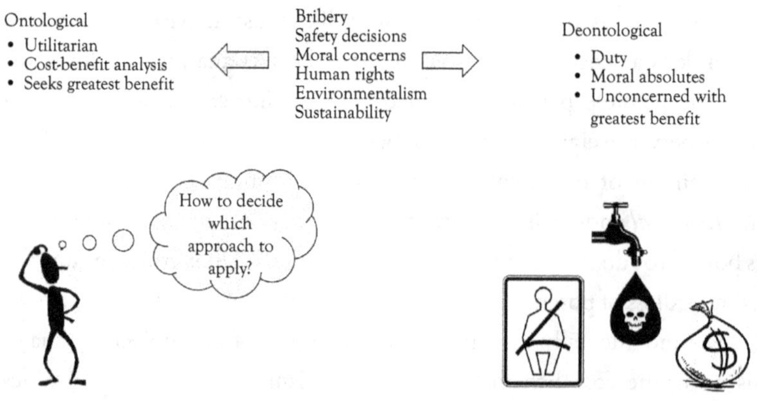

Figure 11.1 Ontological versus deontological ethics

project team may consider an "ethical road map" that identifies specific categories of issues that may arise along with the school of thought to be applied and the corresponding recommended action. Such a document or spreadsheet is likely to produce a consensus within the project team, clarify thinking about behaviors, and finally, reduce the temptation to deviate from ethical norms.

The Corruption Index

Transparency International publishes the Corruption Perception Index (CPI) of every country in the world. The CPI, according to the website, focuses on abuses of power, bribery, and secret deals. The site also indicates that a higher number of journalists have been killed in countries with low CPI scores. The scores therefore provide a general indication of both corruption as well as possible level of safety and security within the country. In addition to publishing the scores, Transparency International also indicates the changes in the scores and makes note of which countries have improved their scores over time. The top five and bottom five country scores from 2016 and 2017 are given in Figure 11.2 (Transparency.org 2019).

Project teams consider the CPI but note that this index measures perceptions rather than actual corruption. If a project team intends to plan and execute a project within a country that is perceived as being high

Top 5-bottom 5 countries corruption perception index

Be careful when operating in countries below mean score 50/100

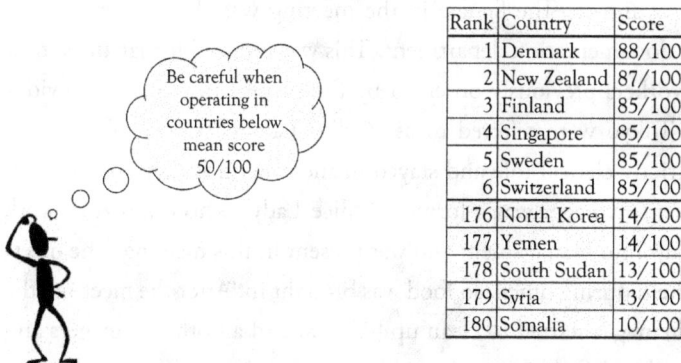

Rank	Country	Score
1	Denmark	88/100
2	New Zealand	87/100
3	Finland	85/100
4	Singapore	85/100
5	Sweden	85/100
6	Switzerland	85/100
176	North Korea	14/100
177	Yemen	14/100
178	South Sudan	13/100
179	Syria	13/100
180	Somalia	10/100

(Transparency International 2019)

Figure 11.2 Corruption Perception Index

in corruption, it is recommended that the project team also confer with the website of the U.S. state department (or other similar government offices within other countries).

Local Versus Universal

Cost–benefit versus "duty" is but one way to analyze ethical behavior in the global project environment. Another is to evaluate practices from the "universal versus relative" approach. An ethical "universalist" will consider that ethical principles apply everywhere. For a universalist, it makes no difference who is exhibiting a behavior—or where it is being carried out. Instead, an act is right or wrong in an absolute sense everywhere. A cultural relativist will insist that it is perfectly acceptable for a cultural practice that is viewed to be appropriate in one culture to be considered inappropriate in another. A relativist makes the ethical determination based upon the cultural context of the act. Consider a scenario that a global project manager may encounter in Japan.

Japan Project Ethical Scenario

A project team member was attending a project review meeting in Tokyo associated with a major infrastructure project. All team members in the room were male, but one was female. The setting was out of the ordinary for the project manager because almost everyone was smoking in this meeting room, a sight rarely witnessed in the United States and many Western countries. The female in the meeting was the manager of the software documentation department. This was unusual for Japan as most female workers previously observed by the project manager in previous visits to Tokyo were referred to as "Office Ladies." Office ladies occupied a strictly clerical role and stayed in the role until they got married. The current manager was a former "Office Lady" who decided to work her way up into management and was present in this meeting. The meeting was held during lunch, so food was brought in. After the meeting, the project manager started to clean up his area, and all other managers and executives had left the room except the female manager. The female manager was cleaning up all the other tables and said, "No, this is my job."

It was clear to the project manager that in Japan even though occasionally a female employee may be promoted, when it came time to clean off tables, it was always the female who had to do it. This practice would never be tolerated in the United States—nor interesting enough—in the People's Republic of China where many top executives are female.

Scenario Summary

In this scenario, the treatment of females differs between the different countries involved in the global project. Which ethical outlook should apply in this case? Is it ethical to treat female employees differently from male employees if the incident takes place within a culture that considers this to be a normal practice? Or, should this be considered an ethical infraction that applies universally? What practices should the project team apply in remote offices within this culture? A reasonable approach to issues such as these is to "never do what does not feel right." Although some ethical differences are a matter of degree, they seek to follow an internal ethical compass while balancing this against the need to avoid offending stakeholders from different cultures.

Ethical Versus Legal

Project managers working in a global project may misunderstand the difference between "legal" versus "ethical." If a global project team follows the law in all cases, should the project team also be considered ethical? The answer to this question is "maybe." While it could be argued that the legal framework of a country encompasses ethical practices, it may be that it does not do so in totality. Further, there have been some instances historically where the law "caught up" with ethical norms years after such practices had been in place. The consideration for global project managers is to not only ensure that project plans fall within the legal framework of all jurisdictions in which the project carries out its work, but to endeavor to go above and beyond to model global expectations for ethical behavior. One example of this concern is the use of "sweatshop" manufacturing operations that are sometimes found in developing regions. The use of such an operation to produce a project deliverable may well fall within the legal framework of the geographically distant location; however, stakeholders from the home country or the global community at large may consider the practice to be unethical.

Ethics, Social Responsibility, and Sustainability

The founder of Panasonic, Konosuke Matsushita, is credited with saying that "it is a crime to fail to make a profit." The rationale behind this saying is that profit demonstrates that the company is satisfying its customers. Further, profit allows the company to pay employees, suppliers, and shareholders of the company. Finally, profit provides the company with the means to pay taxes, which support the well-being of society in general. The Panasonic view is that although it is result of good work rather than an explicit goal, the fundamental purpose of the company is to make a profit. This is consistent with the Friedman view that equates social responsibility (or sustainability) with making a profit. Project managers tasked with delivering a global project will naturally focus on efficient management of the triple constraint so that the project is delivered on schedule and within budget (Figure 11.3).

For the purposes of project management, managing the triple constraint is generally considered to be the primary focus. It is important to keep in mind, however, that from the perspective of local nationals in a less developed country in which the project is being delivered or installed, the strict focus on budgets and return on investment may be viewed as insufficient. It is highly recommended that global project managers be

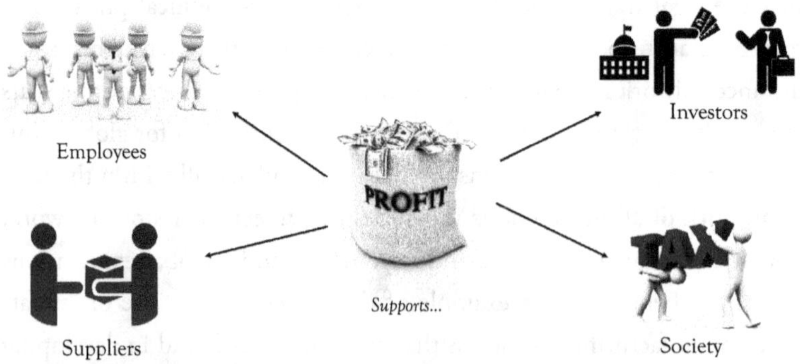

Figure 11.3 Ethics, profit, and sustainability

sensitive to such local concerns and to reach out and support the local community and be observed to do so. Sustainability and social responsibility as a subset of ethical practice in global projects could be considered an advanced form of stakeholder identification, analysis, and engagement. This argues for a more in-depth stakeholder analysis with emphasis on local stakeholders and stakeholder groups at the beginning of global projects.

Revisiting Universal Ethics

There is a natural adjustment between cultures as teams from one culture collaborate and accommodate the commonly accepted ethical practices that differ between teams. What is common in one culture—such as bribery—may be viewed as corruption in another. However, the culture that practices bribery as a way of life might point to the behind the scenes "give and take" that occurs between the Western project and business environment with government. When a government offers a business long-term tax breaks, for example, to bring a major construction project to a specific location, is this a "bribe"? Or is this just negotiation? Perhaps the differences are not so clear-cut in examples such as these. However, there are ethical universal concepts that are not a matter of degree. These include clear-cut criminal behavior, or activities that result in harm to human life.

CHAPTER 12

Closing the Global Project

Formal Client Acceptance

The closure of any project can be ripe for mistakes and miscommunication. Of primary importance in closing the project is obtaining the acceptance of the project deliverables from the client. Often, the client has little incentive to formally accept deliverables early. This is for several reasons. To begin with, since no project deliverable is likely to meet the totality of client requirements, the longer that the client delays acceptance, the greater the likelihood that additional scope in the form of features or enhanced quality of deliverables may be secured. In addition, the typical project will tie client payments to accepted project deliverables. It is common to hold out a final percentage of the total payment to formal acceptance of project deliverables. Any project will require significant negotiation and give-and-take with the client. However, in a global project the final acceptance process will be carried out at a distant geographical location. Final acceptance will likely require intense travel, last-minute "fixes" in software and documentation, and extended work hours on the part of the project team. Complicating final acceptance negotiation is the parallel effort to transition the project deliverables to manufacturing, or in the case of software, production and distribution. Finally, the communication between all parties in this phase of the project is hampered by language and culture barriers in addition to the lack of trust present in geographically distributed global teams. The complexity of the acceptance process in project closure suggests the need for a global project acceptance subproject that is chartered and managed closely complete with targeted milestones (Figure 12.1).

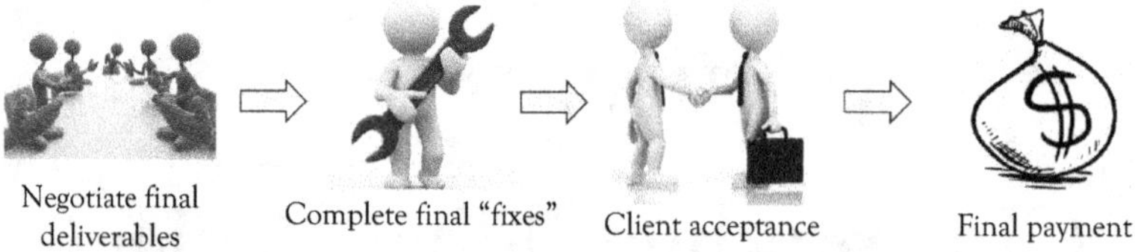

Figure 12.1 Project closure step by step

Release of Resources

The intensity of final acceptance negotiation suggests the need for a "final push" with a maximum number of resources. When acceptance is granted, suddenly many of the resources working on the final deliverables are no longer required. Planning and executing the release of such resources is necessary in any project, but global projects require additional planning and forethought. Some geographically distributed resources may need to continue for a period after acceptance to address any new issues brought forward by the client. Also, some of these resources could be transitioned to a Maintenance of Line (MOL) team. In most projects, the acceptance negotiations include a commitment to add features, fix bugs, or provide follow-up software versions. It is the MOL team that must be chartered to do this, and this team may be a destination for many redundant project team resources. Finally, it is likely that the majority of project team resources around the globe will be released. Team members will be aware of this, and those team members who are the most distant from the head office will tend to be the most concerned. Part of the global project resource plan will include a completion bonus that aids in keeping key team members in place through the formal acceptance of the project and aid in smoothening the transition of the team member out of the project.

Closure of Contracts and Financial Obligations

The release of resources may involve contractors and suppliers of subsystems, software, and documentation. The closure plan outlines how such contracts will be terminated and includes measures for extending supplier support—perhaps in a more limited role—as needed. Contracts may also be associated with equipment rental or leasing, as well as ongoing costs

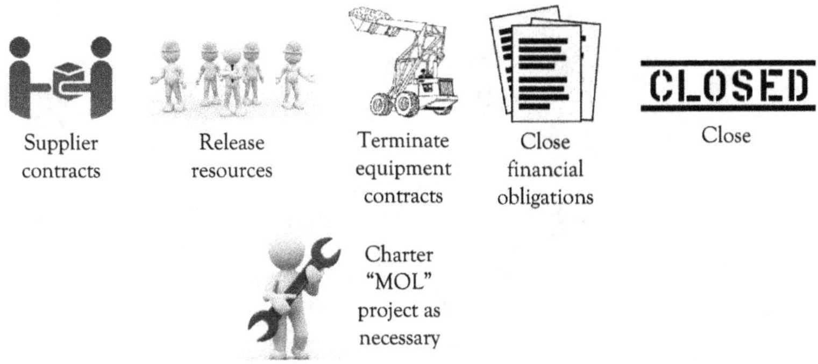

Figure 12.2 Global project and contract closure

for temporary facilities. In a project planned and executed within a single country, these aspects of project closure are straightforward so long as each contract is monitored, tracked, and closed in a timely manner. However, it pays to keep a close eye on the closing out of global financial obligations due to global regulatory, currency, duties, or taxation concerns (Figure 12.2).

PART III

Are Global Projects Really Any Different?

Projects that are run efficiently and managed well follow the due process and pay attention to detail. This outlook on life may be thought of as "good housekeeping." The good housekeeping principle applies in global projects, but the "house" in this case is far larger and it contains many more things to keep track of. This makes the global project "same, but different" in that the same process group activities are carried out, but at the same time, there is much more to think about. To make an analogy with an ongoing operation, many operations today seek to outsource goods and services in order to reduce the cost of doing business, or to gain access to technologies that are not available in the home country. Achieving this is easier said than done. Outsourcing requires additional management expertise, policies, procedures, and processes. Companies that lack these skills may eventually bring back outsourced operations to the home country. Likewise, a project team leading a global project must be capable of succeeding at the effort. This begs the question, "How would the project sponsor, the client, and the project team itself assess its readiness to embark upon the planning and execution of a global project?" One way to approach this is through the concept of the "global project scorecard."

PART III

CHAPTER 13

The Global Project Scorecard

The idea of the global project scorecard is borrowed from Kaplan and Norton's "Balanced Scorecard." The Balanced Scorecard seeks to assess the performance of an organization in a holistic manner rather than on profit and loss alone (Figure 13.1) (Kaplan, and Norton 1992).

The Balanced Scorecard therefore measures company performance in terms of financial measures, internal and external measures (internal processes versus customers), and finally, learning and growth. The global project management scorecard builds on this idea, but rather than capturing performance measures, the scorecard seeks to establish readiness, capability—or said another way—maturity. In this respect, the global project scorecard holds an affinity with the project management maturity model known as OPM3. Maturity models in general could be compared in terms of human development as follows:

Sit: Do we have a process?
Stand: Is it documented?
Walk: Do we follow it?
Run: Does everyone know about it and use it?
Train: Are we optimizing our processes?

The sequence associated with the development of maturity may be a lengthy one. It takes time—beginning from the recognition of the need for process and the development of the process. It is not uncommon for project teams to lack processes for managing projects in the global environment. Developing and growing expertise begins with recognizing what is lacking and then building it.

This corresponds to the OPM3 levels of standardize, measure, control, and continuously improve (Figure 13.2) (Schlichter 2003).

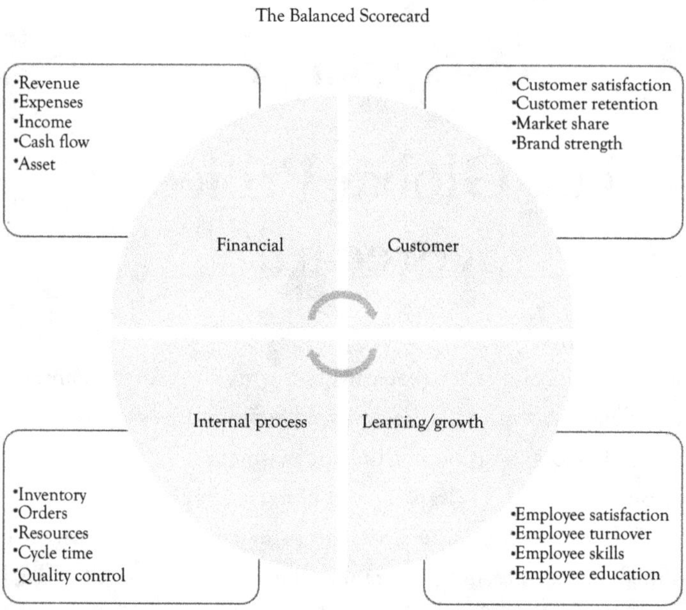

Figure 13.1 The balanced scorecard

The Elements of the Global Project Scorecard

Whereas the balanced scorecard assesses company performance via its financial, customer, internal process, and learning elements, the global project scorecard assesses the capability of the project to plan and execute projects that address the political, economic, social, and technological

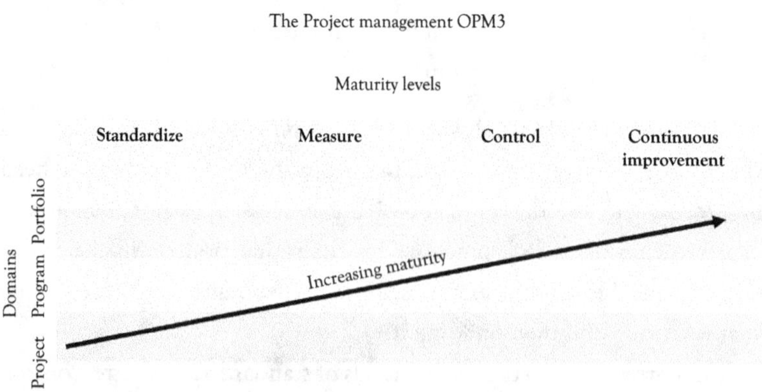

Figure 13.2 Project Management and OPM3

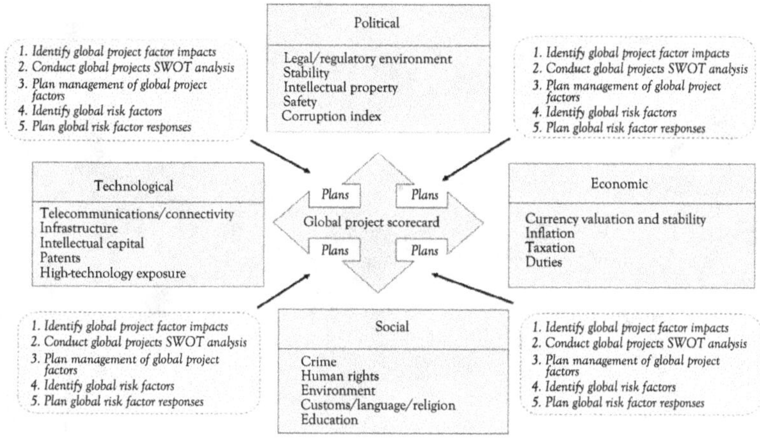

Figure 13.3 Global project scorecard

(PEST) elements of the countries and cultures with which the team will engage. More specifically, the global project scorecard evaluates the ability and process maturity to carry out the five processes of the virtual "Global Project Factor Management Knowledge Area" including the following processes as previously described:

1. Identify the global project factor impacts
2. Conduct a global project SWOT analysis
3. Plan management of global project factors
4. Identify the global risk factors
5. Plan the global risk factor responses

The categories for which a project assesses its global capability is further broken down so that the detail for each PEST category is not overlooked (Figure 13.3).

CHAPTER 14

Assessing the Scorecard

How would a project manager, a sponsor, or a client assess the capability of a project team to plan and execute a global project plan? To begin with, a project team that has experience in managing at least one global project is likely to be more successful than a team that has not previously managed projects in the global environment. However, it may also be the case that the previous project may have succeeded by following ad hoc methods rather than a process-based approach. Because of this, future success is not assured. To improve chances of success, both the client and the sponsoring organization of the project must determine if the project team as constituted is capable of developing and executing a project plan where significant political, economic, social, and technological (PEST) differences exist. An accurate assessment of the global capability of the project team involves the collection and comparison of multiple sources of data to provide a holistic view. Methods for doing this include the following:

Track Record

The global track record assesses previous global projects in terms of the number of projects planned and executed, the scale of the project, and the metrics associated with managing the schedule, budget, and scope given the many global challenges faced by the team. This data may be collected from the project team, or, if in the case of an internal team, pulled from the lessons-learned database (Figure 14.1).

Project Documentation Examination

In addition to the examination of the project track record across several global projects, significant information may be gleaned from the study of project

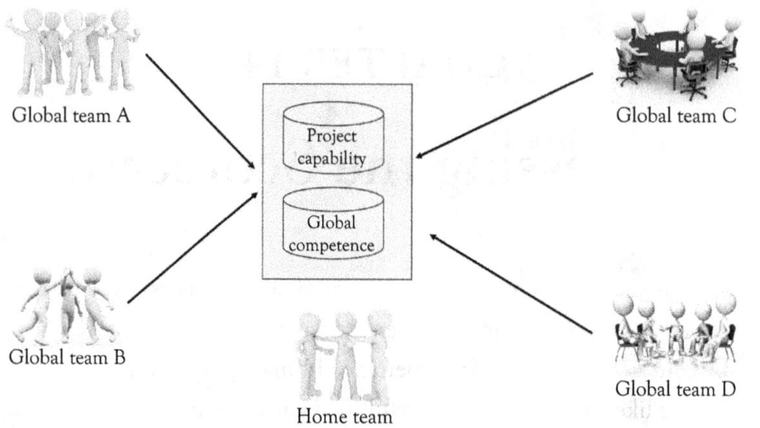

Figure 14.1 Global team track record database

documents sampled from one or more projects previously carried out. Of special interest is the risk register and the degree to which global project factors were addressed. Further, the level of sophistication of the stakeholder analysis and the communications plan would suggest that the team has a strong grasp of the scale of global stakeholders as well as the intensity and complexity of stakeholder engagement and communication (Figure 14.2).

Client Reports

In case where the team has developed and managed previous projects, the team may be evaluated by reaching out to previous clients of the

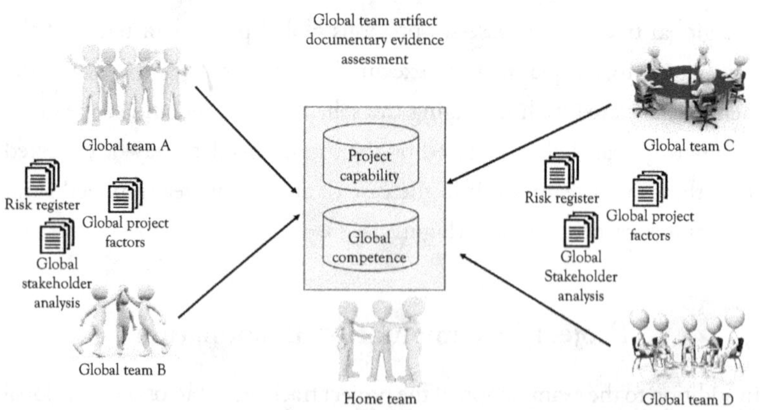

Figure 14.2 Global team artifact assessment

project team. Questions to clients of the project team could include the following:

1. Did the team deliver according to your schedule, budget, and scope expectations?
2. Did the team successfully interact with client team members and stakeholders from other countries?
3. How well did the project team keep you informed?
4. Did the team communicate effectively with stakeholders?
5. Did the team face unexpected risks or financial/regulatory issues?

These are a few examples of the type of questions that would be important to know prior to assigning a global project to the team. Ultimately the sponsoring organization would seek to understand the degree to which the team struggled with managing global project factors.

Internal and External Stakeholder Interviews

Stakeholders within and without the project team, the client, and sponsoring organization can be excellent sources of information regarding the level of expertise of the project team. It is important, however, to seek out stakeholder groups that are likely to have contrasting views on the performance of the project team. For example, not all stakeholders will prove to be supportive of the project team. This is especially the case within large organizations that fund many different project teams as a means of developing and delivering products and executing strategy. A group of stakeholders from a different project team that is competing for funding is likely to be highly critical of other project teams. By way of contrast, other groups of stakeholders within the sponsoring organization and the client may strongly favor the project team and speak highly of its previous track record in managing global projects. It should be kept in mind, however, that the strong and often contrasting opinions of each stakeholder group may reflect the truth of the matter only imperfectly. It is up to the assessor of project team to weigh each source of evidence so that a realistic and accurate view of the project team emerges (Figure 14.3).

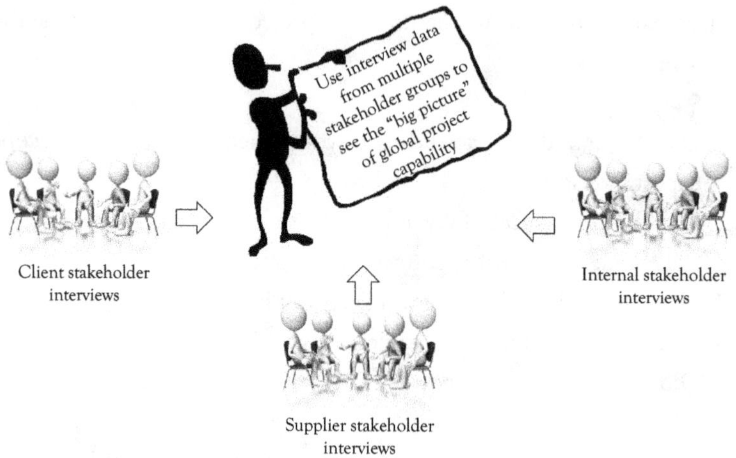

Figure 14.3 Stakeholder interview data collection

Survey Instrument

An overall assessment of global project capability would not be complete without the collection and analysis of significant data collected via a survey instrument. An electronic survey instrument allows for distribution to a large population that includes all stakeholder groups currently in place as well as stakeholders associated with previous global projects. It is useful, however, to use the survey to develop insights into the internal state of readiness of the project team and sponsoring organization, and as well, develop a modified version of the survey to capture the opinion of external stakeholders including the client. An assessment survey may also be used to capture demographic information that identifies the stakeholder groups to which each survey respondent belongs. In this way, the survey data may be used to compare the differences in perceptions of different stakeholder groups regarding the readiness of the sponsoring organization and the project team to undertake global projects.

Although the survey instrument assesses each element of the global project scorecard, the survey first seeks to assess the overall level of global project process maturity using the following series of questions:

Process Maturity Questions

The following survey questions are designed to assess the level of process maturity for managing global projects:

1. The organization has defined policies for chartering global projects.
   Strongly Agree
   ❐ Agree
   ❐ Neither Agree nor Disagree
   ❐ Disagree
   ❐ Strongly Disagree
2. The organization has defined processes for planning and executing global projects.
   ❐ Strongly Agree
   ❐ Agree
   ❐ Neither Agree nor Disagree
   ❐ Disagree
   ❐ Strongly Disagree
3. The organization's global project processes are widely known throughout the organization.
   ❐ Strongly Agree
   ❐ Agree
   ❐ Neither Agree nor Disagree
   ❐ Disagree
   ❐ Strongly Disagree
4. The organization's global project processes are consistently used throughout the organization.
   ❐ Strongly Agree
   ❐ Agree
   ❐ Neither Agree nor Disagree
   ❐ Disagree
   ❐ Strongly Disagree
5. The effectiveness of the organization's global project processes is measured using metrics.
   ❐ Strongly Agree
   ❐ Agree

Process maturity questions	Mean scores	
1. The organization has defined policies for chartering global projects.	>/=3	Good
2. The organization has defined processes for planning and executing global projects.	</= 3	Room to improve
3. The organization's global project processes are widely known throughout the organization.	<3	Lacking maturity
4. The organization's global project processes are consistently used throughout the organization.		
5. The effectiveness of the organization's global project processes is measured using metrics.		

Figure 14.4 Scoring global process maturity surveys

❒ Neither Agree nor Disagree
❒ Disagree
❒ Strongly Disagree

6. The organization's global project processes are consistently used throughout the organization.
❒ Strongly Agree
❒ Agree
❒ Neither Agree nor Disagree
❒ Disagree
❒ Strongly Disagree

The survey is scored using 1 for "Strongly disagree" and 5 for "Strongly agree." Based on this scoring, the level of overall process maturity is assessed as follows (Figure 14.4).

PEST Assessment

The core of the global project scorecard assessment is associated with each of the factors that contribute to the challenge of planning and managing global projects.

I. Political

Legal/regulatory environment

7. The project plan reflects an awareness of the regulatory requirement of the client country.
❒ Strongly Agree
❒ Agree
❒ Neither Agree nor Disagree
❒ Disagree
❒ Strongly Disagree

8. The project plan is evaluated for its alignment with the legal framework of the client country.
   - ❒ Strongly Agree
   - ❒ Agree
   - ❒ Neither Agree nor Disagree
   - ❒ Disagree
   - ❒ Strongly Disagree

Stability

9. The project plan requires an assessment of the likelihood of disruption due to changes in government or government policy.
   - ❒ Strongly Agree
   - ❒ Agree
   - ❒ Neither Agree nor Disagree
   - ❒ Disagree
   - ❒ Strongly Disagree

Intellectual property

10. The project plan includes procedures for safeguarding designs, schematics, and source code.
   - ❒ Strongly Agree
   - ❒ Agree
   - ❒ Neither Agree nor Disagree
   - ❒ Disagree
   - ❒ Strongly Disagree

Safety

11. The project plan includes a travel policy that fosters personal safety while traveling on project business.
   - ❒ Strongly Agree
   - ❒ Agree
   - ❒ Neither Agree nor Disagree
   - ❒ Disagree
   - ❒ Strongly Disagree

Corruption Index

12. The project plan includes a plan to evaluate and respond to reported in-country corruption.
    - ❒ Strongly Agree
    - ❒ Agree
    - ❒ Neither Agree nor Disagree
    - ❒ Disagree
    - ❒ Strongly Disagree

Overall

13. The project risk register and response plan include noted political global factors.
    - ❒ Strongly Agree
    - ❒ Agree
    - ❒ Neither Agree nor Disagree
    - ❒ Disagree
    - ❒ Strongly Disagree

II. Economic

Currency valuation and stability

14. The project budget reflects past currency trends and future projections in the countries in which the project operates.
    - ❒ Strongly Agree
    - ❒ Agree
    - ❒ Neither Agree nor Disagree
    - ❒ Disagree
    - ❒ Strongly Disagree

Inflation

15. The project budget factors in inflation projections for the countries in which the project operates.
    - ❒ Strongly Agree
    - ❒ Agree
    - ❒ Neither Agree nor Disagree
    - ❒ Disagree
    - ❒ Strongly Disagree

Taxation

16. The project budget factors in taxation requirements for the countries in which the project operates.
    - ❒ Strongly Agree
    - ❒ Agree
    - ❒ Neither Agree nor Disagree
    - ❒ Disagree
    - ❒ Strongly Disagree
17. The project plan includes taxation countermeasures for the countries in which the project operates.
    - ❒ Strongly Agree
    - ❒ Agree
    - ❒ Neither Agree nor Disagree
    - ❒ Disagree
    - ❒ Strongly Disagree

Duties

18. The project budget includes import duties for the countries in which the project operates.
    - ❒ Strongly Agree
    - ❒ Agree
    - ❒ Neither Agree nor Disagree
    - ❒ Disagree
    - ❒ Strongly Disagree
19. The project plan includes plans for minimization of import duties for the countries in which the project operates.
    - ❒ Strongly Agree
    - ❒ Agree
    - ❒ Neither Agree nor Disagree
    - ❒ Disagree
    - ❒ Strongly Disagree

Overall

20. The project risk register and response plan include noted economic global factors.
    - ❒ Strongly Agree
    - ❒ Agree

❐ Neither Agree nor Disagree
❐ Disagree
❐ Strongly Disagree

III. Social

Crime

21. The project plan includes an analysis of crime statistics for the countries in which the project operates.
    ❐ Strongly Agree
    ❐ Agree
    ❐ Neither Agree nor Disagree
    ❐ Disagree
    ❐ Strongly Disagree
22. The project plan includes necessary precautions for criminal activity within the countries in which the project operates.
    ❐ Strongly Agree
    ❐ Agree
    ❐ Neither Agree nor Disagree
    ❐ Disagree
    ❐ Strongly Disagree

Human rights

23. The project plan includes an examination of the human rights records for the countries in which the project operates.
    ❐ Strongly Agree
    ❐ Agree
    ❐ Neither Agree nor Disagree
    ❐ Disagree
    ❐ Strongly Disagree

Environment

24. The project plan includes an evaluation of environmental concerns for the countries in which the project operates.
    ❐ Strongly Agree
    ❐ Agree
    ❐ Neither Agree nor Disagree
    ❐ Disagree
    ❐ Strongly Disagree

Customs/language/religion

25. The project plan includes a SWOT analysis to assess the impact of customs, language, and religious observance for the countries in which the project operates.
    - ❐ Strongly Agree
    - ❐ Agree
    - ❐ Neither Agree nor Disagree
    - ❐ Disagree
    - ❐ Strongly Disagree

Education

26. The project plan includes an examination of the level of education in fields related to the project for the countries in which the project operates.
    - ❐ Strongly Agree
    - ❐ Agree
    - ❐ Neither Agree nor Disagree
    - ❐ Disagree
    - ❐ Strongly Disagree

Overall

27. The project risk register and response plan include noted social global factors.
    - ❐ Strongly Agree
    - ❐ Agree
    - ❐ Neither Agree nor Disagree
    - ❐ Disagree
    - ❐ Strongly Disagree

IV. Technological

Telecommunications/connectivity

28. The project plan includes an evaluation of telecommunications and connectivity availability for the countries in which the project operates.
    - ❐ Strongly Agree
    - ❐ Agree
    - ❐ Neither Agree nor Disagree

- ❒ Disagree
- ❒ Strongly Disagree

Infrastructure

29. The project plan includes an evaluation of the business infrastructure for the countries in which the project operates.
    - ❒ Strongly Agree
    - ❒ Agree
    - ❒ Neither Agree nor Disagree
    - ❒ Disagree
    - ❒ Strongly Disagree

Intellectual capital

30. The project plan includes an assessment of the level of available educated workforce for the countries in which the project operates.
    - ❒ Strongly Agree
    - ❒ Agree
    - ❒ Neither Agree nor Disagree
    - ❒ Disagree
    - ❒ Strongly Disagree

Patents

31. The project plan includes an examination of the number of patents secured by the countries in which the project operates.
    - ❒ Strongly Agree
    - ❒ Agree
    - ❒ Neither Agree nor Disagree
    - ❒ Disagree
    - ❒ Strongly Disagree

High-technology exports

32. The project includes an examination of the level of high-technology exports from the countries in which the project operates.
    - ❒ Strongly Agree
    - ❒ Agree
    - ❒ Neither Agree nor Disagree
    - ❒ Disagree
    - ❒ Strongly Disagree

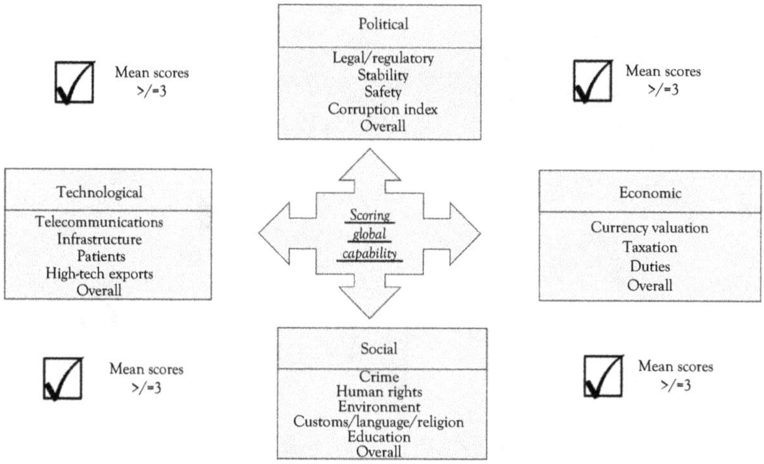

Figure 14.5 Minimum acceptable global capability scores

Overall

33. The project risk register and response plan include noted technological global factors.
    - ❒ Strongly Agree
    - ❒ Agree
    - ❒ Neither Agree nor Disagree
    - ❒ Disagree
    - ❒ Strongly Disagree

Each of the PEST elements are scored from 1 to 5 in the same manner as the overall process maturity assessment questions. Assessment results from each PEST elements fall within a spectrum with a mean score exceeding a mean of 3 indicating a minimum level of acceptable global project readiness for planning and executing global projects (Figure 14.5).

CHAPTER 15

Building Global Project Capability

The result of global project assessment will indicate possible areas for improvement. Knowing which global factors that are not adequately addressed in global project plan is a good beginning. However, the next question is "Where does the global project team go from here?" Recalling the sit, stand, walk, run, train model of process maturity, the first step is to have a process. The process itself may not be ideal, but at a minimum, it is identified and documented. An approach for beginning this effort is to hold a workshop with select project team members as well as select management stakeholders from the sponsoring organization. The workshop would carry out the following activities:

1. *Review global project assessment data*: All collected data including survey results, interviews, and examination of documents is reviewed with the workshop attendees and discussed.
2. *Brainstorming/process identification*: The results of the evaluation of the collected data provides evidence of missing policies, procedures, and processes for planning and executing global projects along with the specific global factors that are unsupported or weakly supported. The workshop attendees use this data to brainstorm and compile a list of missing processes.
3. *Chartering process improvement projects*: The identified "missing pieces" of global project management are then used to charter project teams to develop a corresponding process. Given that process effectiveness is the outcome of maturity, it is acknowledged that strong processes take time to implement and fully develop. Because of this, a recommended beginning is to charter each process improvement

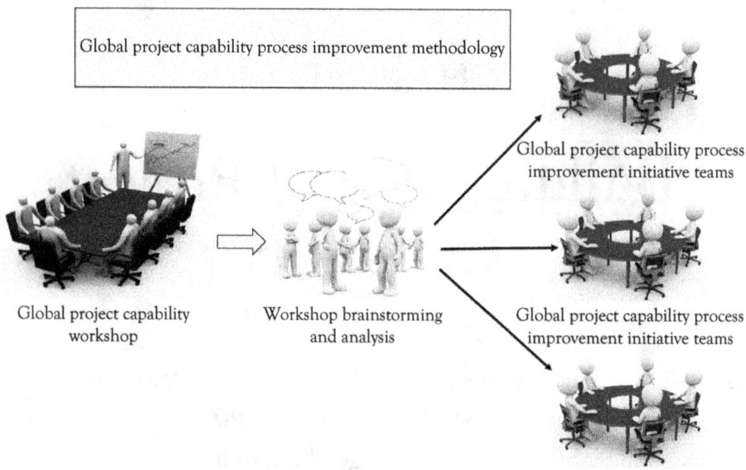

Figure 15.1 Global project capability process improvement

team to develop a template document for project teams to employ as a beginning for establishing an initial process (Figure 15.1).

Standing, Walking, Running, and Training

Once a process is in place in the form of a plan document template, the next step in the maturity model is using the template each time a project is chartered, awareness of the template among multiple project teams, and further the continuous improvement of the process as reflected by the initial template. It is recommended that the process improvement teams that produce the first process template deliverables are used to assess the degree of usage of the templates over time and evaluate the awareness of the process among all global project teams. Further follow-up workshops can be held by the same global project assessment and readiness preparation group for evaluating data on the usage of the new processes, discuss what is working and what is not working, and then identify potential for improvement of each of the process linked to global project factors. Future workshops could follow the very same pattern as the initial workshop that led to the chartering of project teams. For example, a quarterly or semi-annual review of the global project process improvement effort begins with analyzing data on the usage of the process templates including how effective they were. Such reviews also identify areas in which they might be incomplete. Also, each review may collect further data on the level of awareness of processes. It is also of interest in a workshop such as this to consider the degree to which teams may be deviating from the template or modifying it in any way. Once this discussion is taking place, they can be brainstorming among the workshop process improvement teams on what should be improved in the global project plan process templates so that lessons learned from their usage in the existing and previous projects can be incorporated in future projects. The identified improvements can then be used to charter project teams in the same manner as was done initially. The deliverables will be modifications to existing processes or process templates or in some cases complete revisions of previously proposed project plan process templates. After two or three iterations of the process, review is envisioned that the sit, stand, walk, run, train model of process improvement will have reached the "train" status. At this point, the processes could be expected reasonably expected to be fully established and how the global project team does business and the evaluation of global project processes could be folded in two project reviews and be part of the organizational process assets as defined by the PMBOK. Stated in other words, these are documents, templates, policies, procedures, and plans that every project uses. Finally, instead of having a separate set of team members to create implement and assess global project processes, eventually this oversight activity could transition to the project office or other executive governance body within the sponsoring organization (Figure 15.2).

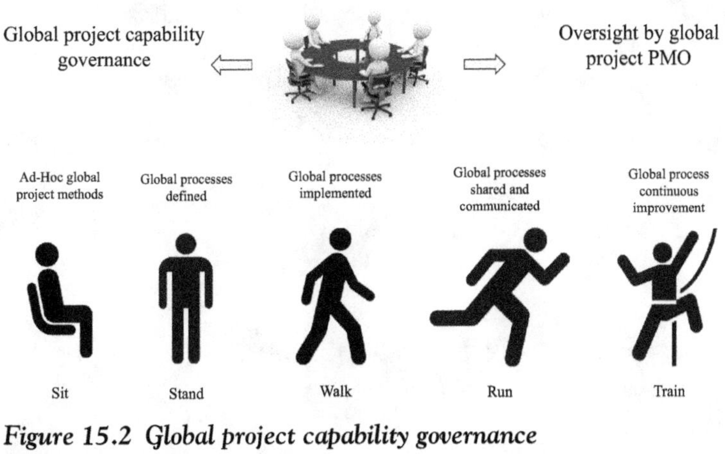

Figure 15.2 Global project capability governance

An outcome of this global project process improvement would be that periodic assessments and forms in the form of data collection from the readiness survey interviews and document studies should produce consistently high compliance scores. In such an environment, global projects would likely experience lower risk and be executed far more efficiently.

Every Project Is Global

There is a strong argument to be made that all projects are global. The vast interconnectedness of the information age in which projects operate today virtually guarantee that at least some global factors will be involved in the project from the conception of the project to its delivery. Project managers today will benefit from this perspective as it will likely lead them to take steps to develop and mature global project management competence in their project management practice. There is no end to the learning and development given the shifting of global alliances and national boundaries, changes in the macroenvironment, and finally the ongoing enhancement of technologies that support global management. Therefore, it is important to seek to incorporate global know-how, incorporate process discipline, and refine and optimize global project practices over time. Such ongoing development is a journey rather than a destination, and the global project scorecard and assessment tools will aid in providing the roadmap.

Appendix

Global Research

Our global economy is complex and ever changing. The following websites are provided as sources to get real-time, accurate status for your personal quest to prepare for a global assignment. The list is not intended to be exhaustive but to highlight sources.

At the time of publishing, these websites were deemed credible. As any user of the Internet should do, evaluate your sources to understand where the information comes from and why it is being communicated.

Organization's Name: Bloomberg BNA

Official website: https://bna.com/

Publicly published purpose and/or mission: Their products provide legal, tax, compliance, government affairs, and government contracting professionals with critical information, practical guidance, and workflow solutions. They leverage leading technology and a global network of experts to deliver a unique combination of news and authoritative analysis, comprehensive research solutions, innovative practice tools, and proprietary business data and analytics. Bloomberg BNA is an affiliate of Bloomberg L.P., the global business, financial information, and news leader.

Organization's Name: Centers for Disease Control and Prevention

Official website: https://cdc.gov/

Publicly published purpose and/or mission: CDC works 24/7 to protect America from health, safety, and security threats, both foreign and in the United States. Whether diseases start at home or abroad, are chronic or acute, curable, or preventable, human error or deliberate attack, CDC fights disease and supports communities and citizens to do the same.

Organization's Name: Commisceo-Global

Official website: https://commisceo-global.com/

Publicly published purpose and/or mission: They provide training and online courses focusing on the insights needed to work with other cultures.

Organization's Name: Constellations

Official website: http://constellations-international.com/

Publicly published purpose and/or mission: Constellations is a consulting agency that creates meaningful interactions to enable better learning, leading, and collaborating for sustainable futures.

Organization's Name: Council on Foreign Relations (CFR)

Official website: https://cfr.org/

Publicly published purpose and/or mission: The Council on Foreign Relations (CFR) is an independent, nonpartisan membership organization, think tank, and publisher dedicated to being a resource for its members, government officials, business executives, journalists, educators and students, civic and religious leaders, and other interested citizens in order to help them better understand the world and the foreign policy choices facing the United States and other countries.

Organization's Name: Doing Business

Official website: http://doingbusiness.org/

Publicly published purpose and/or mission: The Doing Business project provides objective measures of business regulations and their enforcement across 190 economies and selected cities at the subnational and regional level.

Organization's Name: Foreign Affairs

Official website: https://foreignaffairs.com/

Publicly published purpose and/or mission: Foreign Affairs is published by the Council on Foreign Relations (CFR), a nonprofit and nonpartisan membership organization dedicated to improving the understanding of U.S. foreign policy and international affairs through the free exchange of ideas.

Organization's Name: Gallup

Official website: https://news.gallup.com/home.aspx

Publicly published purpose and/or mission: They're a global analytics and advisory firm that helps leaders and organizations solve their most pressing problems.

Organization's Name: TheGlobalEconomy.com

Official website: https://theglobaleconomy.com/rankings/wb_political_stability/

Publicly published purpose and/or mission: TheGlobalEconomy.com serves researchers, academics, investors, and businesspeople who need reliable economic data on foreign countries.

Organization's Name: Global Leadership and Organizational Behavior Effectiveness (GLOBE)

Official website: https://globeproject.com/

Publicly published purpose and/or mission: An organization dedicated to the study of culture, leadership, and organizational effectiveness.

Organization's Name: greenwichmeantime.com

Official website: https://greenwichmeantime.com/

Publicly published purpose and/or mission: Converts the time anywhere in the world.

Organization's Name: The Heritage Foundation

Official website: https://heritage.org/

Publicly published purpose and/or mission: The mission of The Heritage Foundation is to formulate and promote conservative public policies based on the principles of free enterprise, limited government, individual freedom, traditional American values, and a strong national defense.

Organization's Name: Human Rights Watch

Official website: https://hrw.org/#

Publicly published purpose and/or mission: Human Rights Watch defends the rights of people worldwide. We scrupulously investigate abuses, expose the facts widely, and pressure those with power to respect rights and secure justice. Human Rights Watch is an independent, international organization that works as part of a vibrant movement to uphold human dignity and advance the cause of human rights for all.

Organization's Name: International Labour Organization

Official website: https://ilo.org/global/lang--en/index.htm

Publicly published purpose and/or mission: The International Labour Organization (ILO) is devoted to promoting social justice and internationally recognized human and labor rights, pursuing its founding mission that social justice is essential to universal and lasting peace.

Organization's Name: McKinsey and Company

Official website: https://mckinsey.com/about-us/overview

Publicly published purpose and/or mission: They help organizations across the private, public, and social sectors create the change that matters. They do this by embedding digital, analytics, and design into core processes and mind-sets; building capabilities that help organizations and people to thrive in an ever-changing context; and developing excellence in execution to ensure that actions translate into outcomes, quickly and sustainably.

Organization's Name: Transparency International

Official website: https://transparency.org/research/cpi/overview

Publicly published purpose and/or mission: Our Mission is to stop corruption and promote transparency, accountability, and integrity at all levels and across all sectors of society.

Organization's Name: U.S. Department of State

Official website: https://state.gov/travel/

Publicly published purpose and/or mission: The U.S. Department of State leads America's foreign policy through diplomacy, advocacy, and assistance by advancing the interests of the American people, their safety and economic prosperity.

Organization's Name: U.S. Embassy

Official website: https://usembassy.gov/

Publicly published purpose and/or mission: Websites of US embassies, consulates, and diplomatic missions.

Organization's Name: U.S. State Department's Overseas Security Advisory Council

Official website: https://osac.gov/pages/Home.aspx

Publicly published purpose and/or mission: The U.S. State Department's Overseas Security Advisory Council (Council) is established to promote security cooperation between American private sector interests worldwide (Private Sector) and the U.S. Department of State.

Organization's Name: The World Bank Group

Official website: http://worldbank.org/

Publicly published purpose and/or mission: The World Bank Group has two goals: to end extreme poverty and promote shared prosperity in a sustainable way.

Organization's Name: The White House

Official website: https://whitehouse.gov/

Publicly published purpose and/or mission: To follow what is going on politically in the nation's Capitol.

Organization's Name: World Health Organization

Official website: https://who.int/

Publicly published purpose and/or mission: WHO works worldwide to promote health, keep the world safe, and serve the vulnerable. Their goal is to ensure that a billion more people have universal health coverage to protect a billion more people from health emergencies, and provide a further billion people with better health and well-being.

Organization's Name: World Intellectual Property Organization

Official website: https://wipo.int/portal/en/

Publicly published purpose and/or mission: Our mission is to lead the development of a balanced and effective international intellectual property (IP) system that enables innovation and creativity for the benefit of all. Our mandate, governing bodies and procedures are set out in the WIPO Convention, which established WIPO in 1967.

Organization's Name: World Trade Organization

Official website: https://wto.org/

Publicly published purpose and/or mission: The World Trade Organization (the WTO) is the international organization whose primary purpose is to open trade for the benefit of all.

Organization's Name: World Population Review

Official website: http://worldpopulationreview.com/

Organization's Name: World Values Survey

Official website: http://worldvaluessurvey.org/wvs.jsp

Publicly published purpose and/or mission: The World Values Survey (www.worldvaluessurvey.org) is a global network of social scientists studying changing values and their impact on social and political life, led by an international team of scholars, with the WVS association and secretariat headquartered in Stockholm, Sweden.

Bibliography

Gladwell, M. 2008. *Outliers: The Story of Success*. New York, NY: Little, Brown and Company.

Global Alliance for the Project Professions. 2019. "GAPPS: Global Alliance for Project Performance Standards." [online] Available at: https://globalpm standards.org (accessed June 1, 2019).

Hall, E. 1976. *Beyond Culture*. New York, NY: Doubleday.

Hofstede, G. 2003. "Cultural Dimensions." www.geert-hofstede.com

House, R.J., P.J. Hanges, M. Javidan, P.W. Dorfman, and V. Gupta, eds. 2004. *Culture, Leadership, and Organizations: The GLOBE Study of 62 Societies*. Sage publications.

Kaplan, R.S., and D.P. Norton. 1992. *The Balanced Scorecard: Measures that Drive Performance*.

Mintzberg, H. 1979. *The Structuring of Organizations*. Englewood Cliffs, N.J.: Prentice-Hall.

Nscontainer.com. 2019. "FORMS | North Star Container, LLC." [online] Available at: http://nscontainer.com/forms/ (accessed June 1, 2019).

Porter, M.E. 2001. "The Value Chain and Competitive Advantage." *Understanding Business Processes*, pp. 50–66.

Project Management Institute. 2017. *A Guide to the Project Management Body of Knowledge*. (PMBOK guide) 6th ed. Philadelphia, PA: Project Management Institute.

Schlichter, J. 2003. "The Project Management Institute's Organizational Project Management Maturity Model or OPM3." *OPM Experts, LLC* 3, no. 8, pp. 78–81.

Smith, P.B., S. Dugan, and F. Trompenaars. 1996. "National Culture and the Values of Organizational Employees: A Dimensional Analysis Across 43 Nations." *Journal of Cross-Cultural Psychology* 27, no. 2, pp. 231–64.

The Economist. 2019. "Big Mac Index." [online] Available at: https://economist .com/economic-and-financial-indicators/2012/01/14/big-mac-index (accessed June 1, 2019).

Transparency.org. 2019. "Research - CPI - Overview." [online] Available at: https://transparency.org/research/cpi/overview (accessed June 1, 2019).

Velasquez, M.G., and M. Velazquez. 2002. *Business Ethics: Concepts and Cases*, Vol. 111. Upper Saddle River, NJ: Prentice Hall.

Worldvaluessurvey.org. 2019. "WVS Database." [online] Available at: http:// worldvaluessurvey.org/WVSOnline.jsp (accessed June 1, 2019).

Bibliography

About the Authors

Dr. James W. Marion is a tenured associate professor with Embry–Riddle Aeronautical University Worldwide. He is currently the Department Chair of the College of Business Decision Sciences Department. His experience includes leading large organizations in multiple product launches in the United States, Europe, and Asia, as well as significant experience with Japanese companies including NEC and Panasonic. Dr. Marion has a PhD in organization and management with a specialization in information technology management (Capella University). He holds an MS in engineering (University of Wisconsin-Platteville), and an MSc and an MBA in strategic planning as well as a postgraduate certificate in business research methods (The Edinburgh Business School of Heriot-Watt University). He is a certified Project Management Professional (PMP).

Dr. Tracey M. Richardson is a tenured, Associate Professor of Project Management in the College of Business at Embry-Riddle Aeronautical University Worldwide. During Dr. Richardson's 20+ years in the United States Air Force, she had the opportunity to visit over 20 countries, and more than half of the United States, managing the same challenges in operations and logistics, limited resources, and regulation facing large global companies. In various capacities working in aircraft maintenance, including sortie production/operations and backshop industrial manufacturing, Tracey acquired vast leadership skills in all aspects of logistics, operations, production, and talent management. Dr. Richardson has a doctorate of organizational leadership from Argosy University's School of Psychology; master of management, and a bachelor of science in resource management, both from Troy University. She is a certified Project Management Professional and a Project Management Institute (PMI) Risk Management Professional.

Index

Alphabets '*f*' and '*t*' after page numbers indicate figure and table, respectively.

OTHER TITLES IN THE PORTFOLIO AND PROJECT MANAGEMENT COLLECTION

Timothy J. Kloppenborg, Xavier University, Editor

- *Agile Working and the Digital Workspace* by John Eary
- *Passion, Persistence, and Patience* by Alfonso Bucero
- *Adaptive Project Planning* by Louise Worsley and Christopher Worsley
- *The Lost Art of Planning Projects* by Louise Worsley and Christopher Worsley
- *Project Communication from Start to Finish* by Geraldine E. Hynes

www.ingramcontent.com/pod-product-compliance
Lightning Source LLC
Chambersburg PA
CBHW052108230326
41599CB00054B/4911